DAVID Bitton

Monday & Tuesday
8am to 5pm

Wednesday to Friday
8am to 9pm

Saturday & Sunday
10am to 5pm

9519 5111

bittongourmet.com.au

CW00422025

bistro   bread   pastries

DAVID  Bitton

DAVID  Bitton

A French-inspired café cookbook

David Bitton

For Sohani, my partner in business and in life.
You are an anchor and inspiration, always pushing
that little bit harder to help me follow the dream.

Contents

Dessert

Sauces and Sides

Foreword

I well remember meeting a charming fresh-faced young Frenchman back in April 1991. I had been invited to spend a week cooking at The Intercontinental Hotel in Sydney as guest chef at their flagship restaurant, The Treasury. I was hesitant, given the fact that I am not a trained chef, just a country cook. I took the opportunity, as management said, 'for the love of it'. It was also a great way of letting the Sydney public know about the Pheasant Farm Restaurant; times were tight and our business was hanging by a thread due to the economic downturn of the early 1990s.

That fresh-faced young Frenchman was, of course, David Bitton. I soon learned that David had arrived in Australia just five days earlier and, despite jetlag, had virtually come straight from the airport to work in the kitchen. His broad smile and gentle nature were disarming, helping enormously in making me feel okay about being in such a professional kitchen, with my very obvious lack of technique. I remember that week for many reasons; the fact that I burned myself badly late at night coming back to check the ovens when everyone had left the kitchen, that I almost had a catastrophe with a knife wielded by this young chef but, most of all, the confidence I gained in the way David and his executive chef, Gerard, also a Frenchman, accepted me because we spoke the same language — it was about a love of food that transcended 'doing things the proper way'.

David reminded me that I was in the kitchen during that week from 7 in the morning until 11 at night, being my obsessive self, making sure things were prepared and ready. That's what happens in kitchens when everyone cares so much about food.

Over the years I've met up with David several times. When I first saw his tapenade on the market I felt it was a benchmark product. When I discovered he was making it from the café that he began with his wife in November 2000, I knew his success would come. I am delighted by what he has established and achieved.

David's food comes from a deep tradition of his upbringing in France, yet his food encompasses a wider terrain that's accessible to all passionate cooks. I wish him well and always think fondly of the empathy he and his executive chef showed me all those years ago.

— Maggie Beer

My philosophy and approach to food is to provide people with a feeling of coming home, of being able to relax and enjoy their meal in the company of good friends. As a child, my mother would welcome and cook for large numbers of people. Not for a special occasion, instead for the company and enjoyment that comes with the preparing and eating of seasonal produce with friends and family. My cooking comes from that sense of 'open house' where the host welcomes his guests to the table and introduces them to the passion he feels for the produce and in the preparation of dishes. This philosophy is reflected in my Bitton Café and Grocer in the Sydney suburb of Alexandria. People from all walks of life are welcomed at the café and it has become a community hub and sanctuary for people when they drop in for a coffee, meet up with friends, mums and babies catching up for play dates, special occasion lunches or relaxed dinners.

It is in this spirit that my recipes are formed. There is nothing I enjoy more than preparing and serving food to my guests, sitting down with them and enjoying good conversation (along with a great drop of wine, of course).

My formal training is as a chef. This began in France, where I finished my apprenticeship and turned up at my first kitchen job. My first impression? It was hell! However, what began was a lifetime of learning, of facing the unknown and developing a determination to succeed and to continuously learn from my experiences. I'm always learning — from others, from my mistakes, from the experiences that unfold around me.

Food is also about a journey, about discovering new experiences. Impulsively I decided to leave France and make my life in Australia. I was 22 and thought I had experienced the world. I landed in Australia on Anzac Day and started work that day at the Treasury Restaurant in The Intercontinental Hotel. What began was a journey that has taken me to the most unexpected places.

During my career as a chef I have worked around the world and for many five-star restaurants. After 18 years working for others, my wife Sohani and I decided that we wanted to run our own business. To be honest, it was Sohani that pushed me to take the leap. 'Let's open a café?' was the question and she dreamed of making coffees for friendly customers while enjoying good food and a conversation or two. The plan for Bitton Gourmet began. A business partner, Gaby, helped us in our venture. We met when I was working at Sheraton on the Park and he was my apprentice. Gaby has become a member of the family and is with us for every milestone we achieve. Bitton is truly a family-run business.

It hasn't been easy. We eagerly opened a six-table coffee shop in Sydney's inner-west in 2000. The coffee shop next door was thriving; nobody took a step into ours. Sohani and I looked at each other and wondered what we had done, if we had made the biggest mistake in our lives. We had gambled our corporate careers and livelihood on a small café. We decided there were only two options — to give up or work to make our dream come true. Inspired by a quaint shop in Berrima called 'The Little Hand-stirred Jam Shop' we began making our own jams and preserves to use and sell in the café. During the day we worked in the café, at night Sohani and I and a team of chefs I had worked with in the past made jams and preserves in our kitchen (I can still smell the strawberry jam that permeated our apartment constantly). From these humble beginnings a range of jams, sauces and dressings was created; the red-labelled Bitton range of products was born. My dream was that everyone could experience five-star flavours in their home cooking.

Food is not just about eating. It is about memories, it is about influences, it is about enjoyment. Food is about living life and enjoying every moment that comes your way. The recipes in *Bitton* are a mixture of old favourites from the café that I wouldn't dare take off the menu (for fear of my regular customers causing a riot), and food that I love cooking for friends and family. More importantly, these are dishes that are to be shared and to encourage passionate conversation around the dinner table.

David

Introduction

breakfast

Breakfast at Bitton Café is a Sydney institution.

It is welcoming, friendly and a wonderful treat for the most important meal of the day. For seven days a week we have people from all over Sydney, from many walks of life, not to mention our Bitton regulars who have been coming to us for years, start their day with a good coffee and their favourite 'morning' meal. Having breakfast out has become really popular — people can grab something substantial before they head off for a busy work day, families drop by for a leisurely breakfast on the weekend, mums and babies drop in after the bigger kids have gone to school. Having an all-day breakfast is part of the French and Swiss tradition known as *repas suisse*. It is cleansing and simple, providing respite from heavy food. A typical example includes herbal tea, fruit, cheese, good bread, hardboiled eggs and a light cheese dish. This 'breakfast' is more of an evening supper usually enjoyed at a local café. Some of the recipes that follow are Bitton Café favourites that have been a constant on the menu for many years.

Banana Muffins with French Butter and Strawberry and Vanilla Jam

MAKES 10 TO 12

These muffins are whatever you wish for in a muffin because you can adapt this recipe to suit your tastes. Try seasonal fresh fruit or add a couple of handfuls of chocolate chips for a more decadent treat. The suggestion here is to serve these muffins warm with some French butter — a luxurious touch to an everyday breakfast. If you can't get hold of French butter, use the best quality butter you can find. Don't feel that you have to save these muffins for breakfast.

375 g self-raising flour

250 g caster sugar

500 ml milk

250 g butter, melted and cooled slightly

5 free-range or organic eggs

2 ripe bananas, mashed with a fork
 (or season fruit of your choice)

French butter

Bitton Strawberry and Vanilla Jam,
 to serve or your favourite jam

Preheat the oven to 180°C (350°F). Line a 12-hole muffin tin with paper cases.

Sift flour and sugar into a large bowl.

In a glass jug, whisk together milk and eggs. Make a well in the centre of the dry ingredients and add the milk mixture, stirring until the mixture is combined. Add the melted butter, mixing well.

Gently fold in the mashed banana. Spoon the mixture into the muffin trays, filling about three-quarters full.

Bake for 35 minutes or until the muffins are golden and firm to the touch. Test with a skewer and if it comes out clean, your muffins are done.

Serve warm with lashings of French butter and your favourite jam.

Chilli Scrambled Eggs with Wood-fired bread

SERVES 4

Perfect scrambled eggs are a fabulous pick-me-up first thing in the morning. Crunchy toast and a good coffee are the only accompaniments needed. The Chilli Garlic Masala is a kickstart for your tastebuds — chilli and eggs are perfectly paired flavours. This is a favourite Bitton Café breakfast treat that is a nod to my mother-in-laws' enthusiastic use of spice in her cooking.

8 free-range or organic eggs	In a large bowl, lightly whisk the eggs and the cream together with a pinch of salt.
120 ml fresh cream	
Pinch of sea salt	
50 g butter	Heat a non-stick frying pan over high heat.
2 tablespoons Bitton Chilli Garlic Masala or 2 tablespoons of fresh chilli and garlic, finely chopped	Add butter, Bitton Chilli Garlic Masala or fresh chilli and garlic and parsley. Sauté for 1 minute. Add egg and cream mixture to the pan. Cook for 20 seconds or until the egg begins to set around the edge of the pan. Using a rubber spatula, stir the mixture bringing the cooked egg mixture on the outside edge of the pan into the middle. Leave for 20 seconds. Repeat this stirring process until the eggs are just set.
1 tablespoon flat-leaf (Italian) parsley, finely chopped	
4 slices wood-fired bread, toasted and kept warm	
80 g semi-dried tomatoes, thinly sliced for garnish	Place a slice of toasted wood-fired bread on each serving plate.
A small handful of flat leaf parsley, finely chopped	Carefully pile the scrambled eggs on top of the toast.
	Garnish with semi-dried tomatoes and chopped parsley.

Home-made Granola with European-style Yoghurt, Fresh Berries and Orange Jelly

SERVES 4

I have a confession to make. Cereal has never really done it for me at breakfast time as I've never found a cereal that appealed. So I decided to make my own version of granola, a sweet treat of oats, seeds and nuts flavoured with Bitton's renowned Orange Jelly — it adds a touch of toffee to the crunch of the granola. Fresh berries and creamy natural yoghurt make this a breakfast that beats the hell out of your ordinary 'snap, crackle and pop'. During winter you can replace the fresh berries with stewed or poached fruit, such as apples, pears and quinces. You can serve this with a European-style natural yoghurt — at Bitton we dollop spoonfuls of King Island Yoghurt for a special treat.

300 g organic rolled oats

3 tablespoons wholemeal flour

3 tablespoons pumpkin seeds

125 g almonds, lightly toasted

Pinch of salt

3 tablespoons Bitton Orange Jelly or a floral honey

3 tablespoons sunflower oil

200 ml milk, to serve

European-style natural yoghurt, to serve

Fresh berries, such as strawberries, blueberries, raspberries. In winter, use stewed or poached fruits such as apples, pears or quinces, to serve

Bitton Orange Jelly or honey, to serve

Preheat oven to 180°C (350ºF). Line a large flat baking tray (30 cm x 40 cm) with baking paper. Place all dry ingredients into a large mixing bowl and mix well to combine. Add the Bitton Orange Jelly or honey and sunflower oil and mix to evenly coat the dry ingredients.

Tip the mixture out onto the flat baking tray lined with baking paper and spread out evenly. Bake for approximately 10 minutes. Remove from the oven, stir the mixture so that it browns evenly. Return to the oven and bake for another 10 minutes until the mixture smells toasty and is a gorgeous golden brown.

Remove from the oven and cool. Break up any large pieces of granola so that all the pieces are bite-sized. Store in an airtight container if not using immediately.

To serve, place a cup of granola in each serving bowl and pour over fresh milk. Top the granola with natural yoghurt, berries and drizzle over some Bitton Orange Jelly or honey. Serve immediately.

Bitton

Sautéed Forest Mushrooms on Toasted Brioche Gratinated with Gruyère

SERVES 4

This is a simple breakfast dish that uses a combination of different types of mushrooms to really layer the flavours of this dish. Enoki mushrooms are delicate, slender mushrooms that are creamy in colour and add texture to this dish. Shiitake or shimeji mushrooms have a rich 'woodsy' flavour with a meaty texture and add a kick of flavour. The addition of the gruyère cheese makes this perfect comfort food — or a hearty breakfast to help you start the day.

100 g enoki mushrooms

100 g shimeji or shiitake mushrooms

100 g button mushrooms, quartered

100 g oyster mushrooms

125 g butter

1 teaspoon crushed fresh garlic

¼ bunch flat leaf parsley, roughly chopped

Sea salt and white pepper, to season

8 thick slices of brioche

100 g gruyère cheese, grated

Place all the mushrooms in a bowl and toss gently with your fingertips to combine. Place a large frying pan over gentle heat. Add the butter and garlic and cook for a few minutes. Increase the heat and add the mushrooms and parsley. Season with salt and white pepper. Cook the mushrooms for about 4 minutes, stirring them continuously. The mushrooms should be tender and starting to release their juices.

Toast the slices of brioche. Place on a baking tray, divide the mushroom mixture and top each slice. Sprinkle with gruyère cheese. Place the baking tray under a hot grill until the cheese is puffed and golden.

Place two brioche slices on each plate and serve immediately.

Three Cheese Omelette with Organic Ham

SERVES 4

This is a Bitton Café signature dish. It is also a classic French dish that can be eaten for breakfast, as a light lunch or for supper in the evening. An indulgent breakfast that blends the textures of creamy egg, the salty flavours of ham and the ooze of melting cheese. You can use any variation of your favourite cheese to 'customise' your omelette.

12 free-range or organic eggs

150 ml fresh cream

50 g hard blue cheese, crumbled

50 g fresh goat's cheese, crumbled

50 g gruyère cheese, grated

100 g butter, diced

1 tablespoon minced garlic

2 tablespoons flat leaf parsley, finely chopped

100 g organic ham, finely chopped

4 slices grainy bread, toasted and cut into
triangles, to serve

4 tablespoons Bitton Spicy Tomato Sauce
or your favourite tomato relish,
to serve (optional)

Break the eggs into a clean, dry bowl, add the cream and whisk to combine. Divide the egg mixture evenly between four small bowls.

Combine the cheeses in a bowl. Do the same with the garlic, parsley and ham.

Place an omelette pan or a small non-stick frying pan over medium heat and melt 25g butter until foaming. Add a quarter of the garlic, parsley and ham and sauté gently for 1 minute. Tip one bowl of the egg mixture into the pan and swirl to cover the base of the pan. Lift up the edges of the omelette with a spatula and tilt the pan to let the uncooked egg run to the edges of the pan until cooked. It should be slightly golden underneath and a little bit wobbly when pressed with a fingertip.

Sprinkle a quarter of the cheese mixture on the top of the omelette, cook until cheese begins to melt. Fold over one side of the omelette and slide onto a warmed plate. Repeat with the remaining egg, cheese and parsley mixture. Serve with triangles of crunchy toast and Bitton Spicy Tomato Sauce or tomato relish, if using.

Poached Eggs with Tasmanian Smoked Salmon, Baby Spinach on Roesti Potato with Hollandaise Sauce

SERVES 4

Bitton Café is famous for its hearty breakfasts. Here is one that can be either enjoyed with a glass of fresh orange juice and a coffee or ramped up with a glass of Champagne for an indulgent brunch. The roesti potatoes is a versatile Swiss dish that can work as breakfast or as a side serve for dinner.

For the roesti potato:

4 large desiree potatoes (approximately 780 g),
   peeled
150 g clarified unsalted butter, melted and
   cooled slightly
Sea salt and white pepper, to season

1 quantity hollandaise sauce (see page 182)

For the spinach:

1 tablespoon olive oil
4 handfuls of baby spinach, washed
   and well dried

Preheat oven to 50°C (122°F).

To make the roesti potatoes, grate the potatoes into a large bowl. Add the clarified butter and season with salt and white pepper. Mix to combine

Heat a large non-stick frying pan over medium heat. Place four small egg rings into the pan and fill each with the potato mixture. When browned and crisp on one side, remove the egg rings and carefully turn over and cook the other side.

Remove from the pan and place on a lined baking tray, then into the oven to keep warm until required.

Prepare the hollandaise sauce following the method on page 182.

continued on page 32

For the poached eggs:

4 free-range or organic eggs

1 tablespoon white wine vinegar

Pinch of salt

4 slices Tasmanian smoked salmon

6 baby spinach leaves, finely sliced,
 to garnish

For the spinach, heat a large frying pan over medium heat, add the olive oil followed by the baby spinach. Sauté until it wilts slightly, cover and keep warm.

For the eggs, break each egg into a cup to ensure the yolk is intact. Fill a deep frying pan with at least 10 cm of simmering water. Add the vinegar and a pinch of salt to the water. Stir the water with a spoon, creating a small whirlpool. Drop the egg in the centre of this and wait for 3 to 4 minutes. The water will settle and the egg should form an oval. Remove the egg with a slotted spoon, drain and then drop into a pan of cold water. Repeat with the rest of the eggs. To reheat the eggs, slip each egg onto a slotted spoon and hold for 1 minute under simmering water.

To serve, place roesti potato in the centre of each plate. Top with a slice of smoked salmon, then make a bed of spinach on top. Gently place a poached egg on top of each spinach/roesti stack. Spoon over a generous amount of hollandaise sauce, garnish with a sprig of dill and serve immediately.

One-pan Bacon and Eggs with Wood-fired Bread and Spicy Tomato Sauce

SERVES 4

This was one of the first dishes I tackled when I started my apprenticeship on 5 September 1984 in a Paris bistro and café that also had guest rooms upstairs. I was 15, had just left home and was faced with cleaning garbage bins, sweeping the hotel car park and working in the cold larder in the cold and wet weather. I worked seven days in the kitchen and my apprenticeship was also a lesson in life in the real world.

12 rashers organic short-cut bacon, rind removed

8 free-range or organic eggs

Sea salt and white pepper, to season

4 slices wood-fired bread, toasted, to serve

Bitton Spicy Tomato Sauce or your favourite tomato relish, to serve

Place a small frying pan over a medium high heat and add three rashers of bacon. Cook the bacon until the fat is released into the pan and the bacon starts to become crispy. The idea of this dish is to cook the eggs in the bacon fat. Season with salt and white pepper.

Break two eggs into the pan and cook to your liking. If you prefer the yolks to be well cooked, finish off the eggs under a hot grill. Slide this onto a toasted slice of wood-fired bread and keep warm.

Repeat the above steps with the rest of the bacon and eggs.

Finish off the dish with some Bitton Spicy Tomato Sauce or your favourite tomato relish.

Note: *For a vegetarian option or an added treat, you can sauté 100 g button mushrooms in butter with a teaspoon of finely chopped garlic and parsley. Cook until soft and the liquid released from the mushrooms is reduced by half.*

Bitton

French Toast à la Bitton with Fresh Strawberries and Orange Jelly

SERVES 4

The original version of French toast is *pain perdu* or 'lost bread'. It is a French recipe that dates back to medieval times. Used by the poorer people to use up their stale bread, it was a special treat served at the end of the week. Eggs, cream and vanilla along with the traditional dusting of cinnamon sugar is a mainstay with this dish. I like to mix things up by adding fresh seasonal fruit and a drizzle of Bitton Orange Jelly. Eating 'lost bread' has never tasted so good.

4 free-range or organic eggs

100 ml cream

1 vanilla pod, split, scraped and seeds set aside

4 tablespoons caster sugar

4 tablespoons ground cinnamon

8 tablespoons clarified butter

8 thick slices white wood-fired bread
(better to be two to three days old)

150g strawberries, sliced, to serve

6 mint leaves, finely sliced (optional)

4 tablespoons Bitton Orange Jelly
or maple syrup

Whisk the eggs, cream and vanilla seeds together and pour into a flat dish. Combine the caster sugar and cinnamon in a separate bowl.

Place a non-stick frying pan over medium heat and melt a tablespoon of clarified butter.

Dip a slice of wood-fired bread into the egg mixture and let it soak for a minute or two. Make sure it doesn't get too soggy and fall apart. Dust on both sides with the cinnamon sugar. Place the bread into the heated pan and fry on both sides until golden brown. Remove and set aside in a warm place. Repeat with the rest of the bread, egg mixture and clarified butter.

Combine the sliced strawberries with the mint (if using) in a serving bowl.

To serve, place two slices of French toast onto each plate and drizzle with Bitton Orange Jelly or maple syrup.

Bitton

entrée

An entrée is an appetite teaser, traditionally a small dish such as soup or a salad. It is designed to be light, filled with clean flavours to prepare you for the more substantial main dish. The recipes here can be served as entrées or light meals — such as lunch or supper when eating something heavier doesn't seem to fit the bill. During my time working in Switzerland I was given the vegetable station and had to come up with three different vegetable dishes to go with each meal. I learnt very quickly how to be creative and come up with as many variations as possible as I couldn't serve the same vegetable dish twice. Having to be inventive paid off and my cooking repertoire expanded, allowing me to play around with a lot more flavours and textures. This experience is reflected in my approach to the entrées in this section. There is a mix of salads and seafood; all are simple to prepare and very easy to eat! There are lots of ideas for different ways to prepare vegetables. Included in this section are Bitton Café staples, some classic French recipes such as soup a L'oignon, my mum's cheese tart and dishes that I love to cook for my family and friends.

Entrées

Prawn Cocktail

SERVES 4

Everybody secretly loves a classic prawn salad. There is something retro in this dish that appeals to memories of first trying prawns — served cold with a tangy, salty mayonnaise. Marie Rose Sauce is basically ketchup blended with mayonnaise. My addition of cognac pushes this sauce towards being something quite special. The cayenne pepper adds a perfect touch of spice to the dish.

12 to 16 cooked, peeled and deveined prawns

**4 radicchio leaves, washed and trimmed
  slightly to form a cup**

$1/2$ iceberg lettuce, finely shredded

3 tablespoons Marie Rose Sauce (see page 184)

1 lemon, cut into eights

On each serving plate, place a radicchio leaf 'cup'. Divide the shredded iceberg lettuce evenly among the radicchio cups and arrange three or four prawns on top. Drizzle with Marie Rose sauce and serve with lemon wedges.

Duck Salad with Witlof, Endive and Walnuts

SERVES 4

This is an easy and impressive salad to serve to your guests. Duck is a rich meat that needs to be tempered with sharp flavours. Witlof is a white leafed vegetable that was discovered quite by chance in Belgium in the mid 19th century. It is also known as endive or chicory. Curly endive is a curly leafed vegetable that has a slightly bitter flavour. It works wonderfully with the duck and the walnuts.

4 duck breasts, skin on

2 witlof bulbs, washed, dried and leaves separated

150 g curly endive, washed and dried

80 g walnuts

1 red onion, halved and finely sliced

sea salt and white pepper, to season

Bitton Dressing or French vinaigrette (see page 174), to taste

Preheat oven to 220°C (425°F).

Place an ovenproof medium frying pan over high heat. Sear the duck breasts, starting with skin side down for about 3 to 4 minutes. Turn over and sear for the same amount of time on the other side.

Place in oven for 8 minutes. Remove duck breasts and rest on a rack set over a dish to catch the juices. Reserve.

In a large bowl, place witlof leaves, curly endive, walnuts and onion. Season well and toss lightly with your fingertips.

Finely slice the duck breasts and add to the salad. Drizzle over some of the duck juices. Add Bitton Dressing or French vinaigrette and mix thoroughly.

To serve, divide among 4 plates.

Vegetable Risotto with Caramelised Eggplant

SERVES 4

A simple yet glamorous vegetarian dish that uses fresh vegetables to their best advantage. You can serve this depending on your mood or occasion. Serve the risotto in a bowl topped with the caramelised eggplant as a comforting meal or stack (using an egg ring) and garnish with Bitton Coriander Pesto for a drop-dead gorgeous dinner party dish. Although not a difficult dish, risotto needs your full attention as you need to stir it constantly for about 20 minutes. This dish is a favourite with both vegetarians and carnivores.

For the caramelised eggplant:

1 medium eggplant

$^1/_2$ bunch thyme, leaves finely chopped

2 sprigs rosemary, leaves finely chopped

200 ml balsamic vinegar

2 tablespoons brown sugar plus an extra
  2 tablespoons

1 tablespoon sea salt

Pinch of white pepper

100 ml oil

For the vegetable risotto:

500 ml good quality vegetable stock

50 g butter

50 ml olive oil

1 white onion, finely diced

$^1/_2$ clove garlic, finely chopped

Preheat oven to 150°C (300°F).

To make the caramelised eggplant, slice the eggplant into 1 cm thick rounds. Score the flesh with a sharp knife. Salt well and place in a colander for about an hour. Remove from colander and drain off any excess liquid. Rinse the eggplant slices and set aside.

In a large metal bowl combine the thyme, rosemary, balsamic vinegar, two tablespoons of sugar, salt and white pepper. Pour in the oil in a slow, thin stream whisking continuously. When all the oil is added, dip the eggplant slices into the oil mix and place on a baking tray lined with baking paper. Sprinkle with the extra two tablespoons of sugar. Bake for 25 to 35 minutes until the eggplant is golden brown and caramelised around the edges. Remove from oven, set aside and keep warm.

To make the vegetable risotto, heat vegetable stock in a saucepan. In a heavy-based deep frying pan, melt the butter and add the oil over

continued on page 48

200 g arborio rice

1 carrot, peeled and diced

$^1/_2$ celery stalk, diced

1 leek, white part, finely diced

250 ml white wine

50 g parmesan, grated

16 leaves baby spinach, washed

2 tablespoons fresh corn kernels

2 roma tomatoes, seeded and finely diced

1 zucchini, finely diced

4 tablespoons Bitton Coriander Pesto
 or your favourite herb pesto, to serve
Fresh coriander leaves, for garnish

gentle heat. Add the onion and sauté for a few minutes. Add the garlic and continue cooking until the onion is soft. Add the rice and raise the heat to moderate. Stir to ensure rice is evenly coated with butter and oil and begins to look slightly translucent. Add the diced carrot, celery and leek and cook until they are slightly softened. Add the wine while continuously stirring the rice and the vegetables.

When the wine is absorbed by the rice, add a ladleful of hot stock. Turn down the heat to a high simmer. Keep adding ladlefuls of stock, stirring and allowing each ladleful to be absorbed before adding the next one. This will take about 20 minutes.

Taste the rice to see if it is cooked. Continue adding the stock until the rice is *al dente* — the rice is soft with a slight firmness or bite to it. Check the seasoning. Stir through parmesan, baby spinach leaves, corn kernels, tomatoes and zucchini.

To serve, place one caramelised eggplant round on each serving plate, top with a couple of spoonfuls of risotto, then place another eggplant round on top. Drizzle the Bitton Coriander Pesto or your favourite pesto around the outside of the stack and garnish with fresh coriander leaves.

Bitton

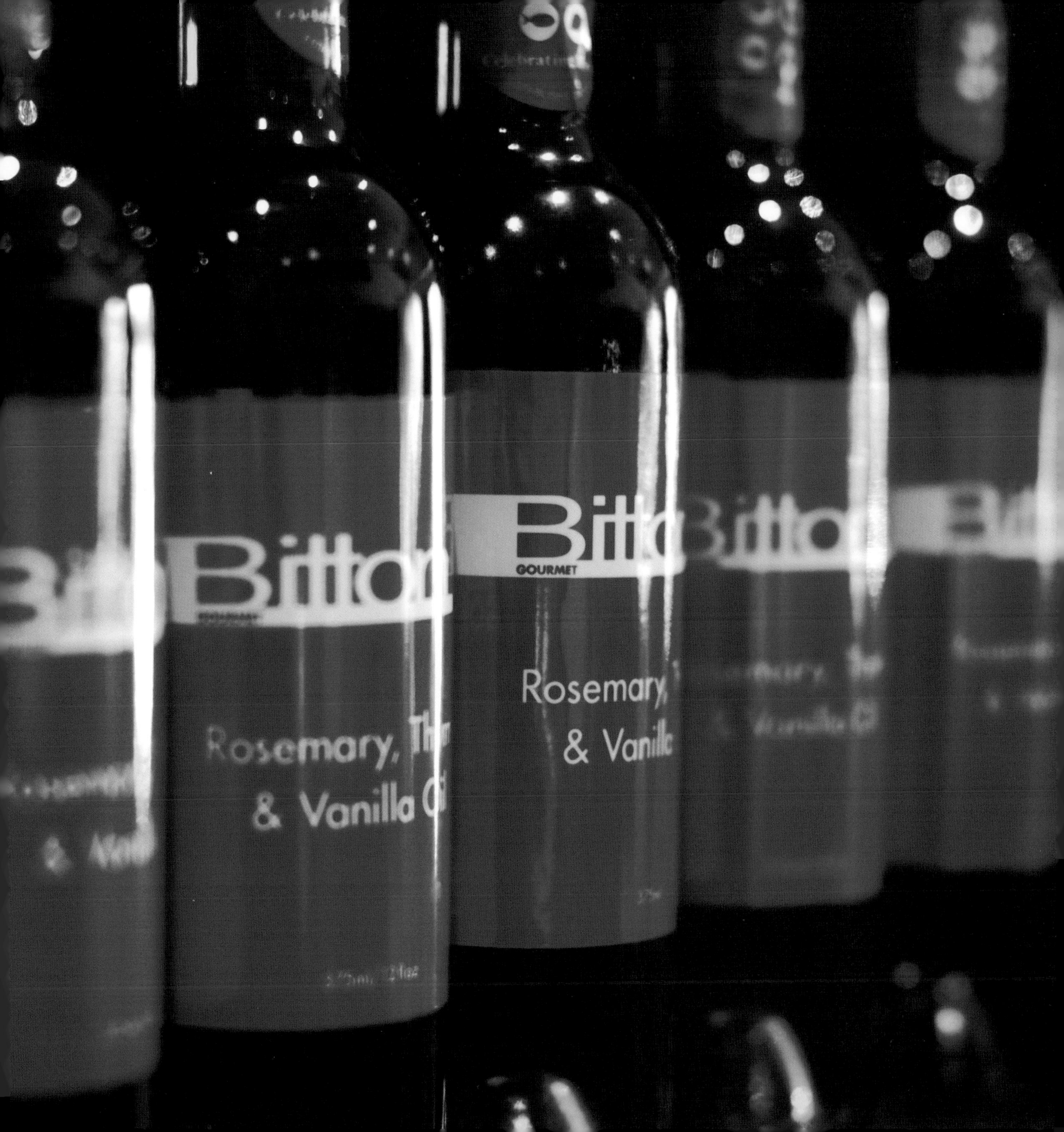
Bitto
GOURMET
Rosemary,
& Vanilla
& Vanilla Oil

Pacific Oysters with Wilted Spinach and Horseradish Sabayon

SERVES 4

This is a dish that was served during my time at Gekko. As oysters are seasonal, included on the menu was an oyster dish that reflected winter and summer. This more of a 'winter' oyster dish but it can be eaten anytime you fancy oysters on the menu.

For the horseradish sabayon:

200 g clarified butter

3 free-range or organic egg yolks

2 tablespoons white wine vinegar

1 tablespoon horseradish cream

Sea salt and white pepper, to taste

12 Pacific oysters, freshly shucked

50 g baby spinach, wilted slightly in a hot pan

For the sabayon, place the egg yolks and the vinegar in a bowl over a large saucepan of boiling water. Whisk continuously until the mixture becomes pale and thick. When it is the right consistency it will hold the figure of eight when drawn in the mixture with the whisk. To prevent the mixture from getting too hot and becoming scramble eggs, hold onto the bowl and when it becomes too hot to handle, remove from over the boiling water. Continue whisking until the bowl cools and then replace over heat. Repeat as often as is need to thicken the sauce.

Remove from heat and slowly add the clarified butter whisking constantly until combined. Whisk in the horseradish cream. Set aside until required.

Remove each oyster from its shell. Divide the wilted spinach equally among the oyster shells and replace the oyster. Spoon a generous amount of the sabayon over each oyster.

Preheat grill to hot and place oysters onto a baking tray and grill until the sauce is a light golden brown. Serve immediately on a plate covered with rock salt.

Grilled Scallops with Balsamic Vinegar, Parmesan and Asparagus

SERVES 4

This is five-star simplicity on a plate. It is light and healthy without cutting back on flavour. You don't need major cooking technique as the ingredients — scallops, parmesan and asparagus — speak for themselves. The balsamic reduction is something a little special that brings together the fresh flavours. It is also a great sauce to drizzle on your favourite vegetables. If you don't have time to do the reduction you can substitute with a good quality balsamic vinegar that is thick and syrupy.

16 asparagus spears (white if in season)

8 cherry tomatoes, halved

100 g mixed salad

4 tablespoons Bitton Lemon Dressing
 or French vinaigrette (see page 174)
 plus extra for serving

16 scallops, coral removed

Sea salt and white pepper, to season

Olive oil for cooking

Reduced balsamic vinegar (see page 192)

80 g parmesan, shaved

Prepare the asparagus by exerting gentle pressure at the base of each spear until it breaks where it is tender. Place in boiling water for 3 to 4 minutes or until still slightly firm. Drain and refresh under cold water.

Combine the asparagus, cherry tomato halves and salad leaves in a bowl. Add the Bitton Lemon Dressing or French vinaigrette and toss gently. Arrange the salad on four plates.

Prepare the scallops by patting dry with paper towel and seasoning with salt and white pepper. Place a heavy chargrill pan over high heat, brushing it lightly with olive oil. Place the scallops on the chargrill pan. Cook each side for half a minute. Remove, set aside and keep warm.

Place four scallops on each serving plate and top with a small handful of dressed salad. Drizzle over reduced balsamic vinegar and garnish with shaved parmesan.

Soupe a L'oignon

SERVES 8

This is a classic French onion soup that sounds much better in its native language. Legend has it that the soup was invented by Louis XV. Coming back late at night to his hunting lodge, Louis was hungry yet discovered he only had onions, butter and champagne in his provisions. Essentially this is a modern version of a French dish that has been eaten by farming people since the 17th century when onions were easy to grow and were plentiful. A warming dish for a cold night.

100 g butter

2 kg brown onions, peeled and sliced thinly

2 garlic cloves, peeled and chopped

$1/4$ bunch thyme, leaves finely chopped

2 sprigs rosemary, leaves finely chopped

1 tablespoon flour

3 litres good quality vegetable stock, heated

For the croutons:

1 baguette

1 head garlic, cut in half horizontally

60 g butter, melted

100 g gruyère cheese, grated

Sea salt and white pepper, to season

Place a large heavy-based stockpot over low heat. Add the butter, then the sliced onions and sauté for about 20 minutes until soft and translucent. Add the chopped garlic, thyme and rosemary and continue cooking until the onions begin to become golden brown and very soft. This will take up to 30 minutes. Stir the onions continuously. Sprinkle over the flour and cook, while stirring, for a further 5 minutes.

Add the hot vegetable stock to the onion/flour mixture. Continue stirring to avoid the flour from becoming lumpy. Cover and cook for 30 minutes on low heat. The onions should be tender, almost melting into the liquid. Season with salt and white pepper.

To make croutons, rub the garlic over the baguette, slice, then brush with melted butter. Sprinkle each slice of bread with grated gruyère cheese, place on a baking tray and put under a hot grill until the cheese is melted and golden.

Ladle the soup into eight bowls and float a crouton on top. This can also be served from one large soup tureen.

Mum's Cheese Tart

SERVES 4

This tart was our childhood version of macaroni cheese! Mum made this tart regularly, serving it straight from the oven, accompanied by a green salad. The shortcrust pastry was always freshly made and melted in the mouth. The cheese filling is light and fluffy. A simple meal that sums up the essence of classic French cookery. The ingredients must be of the best quality. A good quality bought pastry can be used if you don't have time to make your own.

1 sheet of good quality shortcrust pastry (such as Carême) rolled out to fit a 22cm/23cm flan tin

100 g washed rind cheese, cut into thin slices

100 g goat's cheese, cut into thin slices

50 g blue cheese, cut into slices

80 g cheddar cheese or gruyère cheese, grated

2 eggs

2 egg yolks

200 ml crème fraiche

150 ml pouring cream

Pinch of freshly grated nutmeg

Sea salt and white pepper, to season

Preheat oven to 200°C (390°F).

Place the pastry into the greased flan tin, press gently into the corners and trim.

Cover the base of the tart with the cheese slices, layering it evenly.

In a bowl, whisk the eggs, egg yolks, crème fraiche and pouring cream together. Add nutmeg and season with salt and white pepper. Pour this over the cheese-covered pastry base.

Sprinkle the grated cheddar or gruyère over the top and bake in the oven for 30 minutes.

Serve warm with a green salad and a glass of chilled white wine.

Wood-fired Sourdough Bread with Vine-ripened Tomatoes, Goat's Cheese and Basil Oil

SERVES 4

This is the ideal dish to serve for a light lunch or as part of an antipasto plate before a main meal. The basil, tomato and goat's cheese is a perfect combination that captures the essence of sitting in the summer sun, sipping a crisp white wine while looking out across the water.

For the basil oil:

100 g basil

100 g baby spinach

1/2 bunch flat leaf parsley, stems removed, roughly chopped

200 ml olive oil

Sea salt and white pepper, to season

4 slices sourdough bread

2 vine-ripened tomatoes, sliced

50 g goat's cheese

Sea salt, to season

To make the basil oil, place a large saucepan filled with water over high heat. Bring to the boil. Place the basil and spinach in a sieve and drop in boiling water for 30 seconds. Plunge into cold water. Remove and drain well. Place the blanched basil and spinach with parsley, olive oil and salt and white pepper in a blender or food processor and blend for a minute.

Toast the sourdough bread and place each slice on a serving plate. Top with sliced tomatoes. Crumble goat's cheese over the top, drizzle generously with basil oil and add a little sea salt to season.

Mushroom and Vanilla Cappuccino Soup

SERVES 4

Vanilla is usually associated with sweet dishes. In my version of 'cream of mushroom soup', the subtle hint of vanilla enhances the earthy flavour of the mushrooms. This elegant soup is perfect for any dinner party or if you want to treat yourself and spice up a cold winter's night. For a decadent and impressive treat you can either top this with a cappuccino froth or drizzle with truffle oil.

3 tablespoons Bitton Rosemary, Thyme and Vanilla Oil (or in a cup of olive oil steep a split vanilla pod and a sprig of thyme for 30 minutes)

1 brown onion, peeled and finely chopped

1 garlic clove, finely chopped

250 g button mushrooms or Swiss brown mushrooms, finely sliced

250 ml dry white wine

750 ml vegetable stock

250 ml fresh cream

Sea salt and white pepper, to season

For the cappuccino froth:

125 ml light milk

Freshly grated nutmeg or ground cinnamon, for dusting

Place a large frying pan over medium heat. Add Bitton Rosemary, Thyme and Vanilla Oil. Add the onion and garlic and cook until translucent.

Add the sliced mushrooms to the pan and cook, stirring occasionally, until they are soft. Add the white wine and reduce by half. Add vegetable stock and reduce by half. Increase the heat to high and bring to the boil. Boil for 10 minutes until the liquid has reduced by a third. Place the mushroom mixture in a food processor and process until smooth. Pour the soup into a deep saucepan and place over high heat. Add the cream and bring the soup to the boil.

Remove from heat and season to taste. Serve in warmed soup bowls or latte glasses alongside crusty bread and a green salad.

For the cappuccino froth, in a bowl placed over a saucepan of boiling water pour in the milk, heat gently and whisk until frothy. Float the froth on the top of the soup and lightly dust with nutmeg or cinnamon.

Chilli Garlic Masala Prawns with Couscous Salad

SERVES 4

'Masala' is a term used in South Asian cuisines to describe a mixture of spices used to flavour a dish. This dish uses a garlic-based masala that echoes my wife Sohani's Indian heritage. The taste combination of the garlic and chilli, juicy mango and a flavour blast of fresh herbs will put the sizzle in any summer entertaining you might be planning.

For the prawns:

48 large green Australian prawns, peeled,
  deveined and tails left on

2 tablespoons Bitton Chilli Garlic Masala or
  2 tablespoons chilli and garlic, finely chopped

2 tablespoons olive oil

Sea salt, to season

For the salad:

50 g couscous

100 ml water

sea salt, to taste

1 tablespoon olive oil

1 large tomato, diced

1 red onion, finely chopped

1 mango, peeled and diced

1 bunch coriander leaves only, washed

Juice of 1 lemon

Fresh lemon wedges, to serve

Baby herbs, to garnish

Place the prawns into a large ceramic bowl and add the Bitton Chilli Garlic Masala or fresh chilli and garlic, olive oil and sea salt. Mix well to coat the prawns. Cover the bowl and place in the fridge to marinate for 2 hours or overnight.

For the salad, place a small saucepan over high heat, add water and bring to the boil. Add some sea salt to taste and a tablespoon of oil. Place the couscous in a small bowl and pour the boiling water over the top. Cover and let stand for about 5 minutes until all the water is absorbed. Fluff up the couscous with a fork, set aside in a warm place. When ready to serve, add the tomato, onion, mango and coriander to the couscous, combine well.

Pre-heat the barbecue or frying pan. Place the prawns onto the barbeque and cook for 2 to 3 minutes. Turn and cook for a further 3 minutes. Add a squeeze of lemon to the prawns when you finish cooking them.

To serve, place a mound of couscous salad on each plate, top with three or four prawns and garnish with a lemon wedge and baby herbs. You can also use an egg ring to form a neat stack.

Bitton

Glazed Quail with Spiced Apple Stir-fry

This dish might sound unusual, but the rich flavour of the quail is lifted by a fruit stir-fry that echoes the distinctive flavours of South-East Asia. The combination of apple, passionfruit, coriander and ginger are the perfect partners to the burnished beauty of the quail. An easy yet surprising dish to bring to your dinner table. Chicken breasts with the skin left on can be used instead of the quail. This dish can be served on individual plates. It also looks impressive served from a large platter, garnished with baby herbs.

For the spiced fruit stir-fry:

2 tablespoons Bitton Chilli Oil
 or a good quality chilli oil

4 granny smith apples, peeled, sliced thinly

1 tablespoon of ginger, freshly grated

1 tablespoon caster sugar

1 passionfruit, pulp and seeds only

$1/2$ bunch coriander, roughly chopped

Sea salt and white pepper, to season

For the quail:

8 quail breasts

2 tablespoons olive oil

2 tablespoons Bitton Asian Dressing
 or sweet soy sauce

A small handful of baby herbs, washed
 and picked, for garnish

Preheat the oven to 200°C (390°F).

Place a shallow frying pan over a medium to high heat. Add Bitton Chilli Oil or chilli oil. Place the apples in the pan and stir-fry for 30 seconds. Add the ginger, caster sugar, passionfruit pulp, coriander and season with salt and white pepper. Cook the apple mixture on high for another 30 seconds.

For the quail breasts, place a small non-stick frying pan over medium to high heat. Add the olive oil and sear the quail breast skin side down for 1 to 2 minutes. Turn over and sear for the same amount of time until coloured. Place the quail in a baking dish and place in the oven for 3 to 4 minutes or until cooked. You can test this by pressing your finger against the thickest part of the quail breast. If the flesh springs back when lightly touched, it is cooked. Remove from oven and drizzle with Bitton Asian Dressing or sweet soy sauce.

To serve, divide the apple mixture evenly between four plates. Arrange two quail breasts on top and drizzle over the sauce. Garnish with baby herbs.

WA Sardines with Confit Tomatoes, Sourdough Bread and Mozzarella

SERVES 4

This is an Italian twist on the old-fashioned TV snack of sardines on toast. Add some roasted and caramelised tomatoes, some buffalo mozzarella and you have a dish that doesn't need to be eaten in front of the TV at all. Serve it up as a light lunch dish or something more substantial to serve with drinks. Take the time to reduce the balsamic vinegar. You will end up with a sweet and sour syrup that can be used in other dishes as a sauce or salad dressing.

For the confit tomatoes:

8 roma tomatoes, halved lengthways

4 tablespoons olive oil

4 sprigs thyme

Sea salt and white pepper, to season

4 thick slices sourdough bread

4 balls buffalo mozzarella, thinly sliced

8 WA sardine fillets, canned in brine

1 tablespoon Bitton Chilli Oil or good quality chilli oil

Reduced balsamic vinegar (see page 192)

Small handful of onion sprouts, for garnish

For the confit tomatoes, preheat the oven to 180°C. Placed the halved tomatoes, cut side up on a baking tray, drizzle with oil, sprinkled with salt and white pepper and sprigs of thyme. Cook for 30 to 40 minutes until the tomatoes are soft and caramelised around the edges.

Toast the sourdough bread and place each slice on a serving plate. Top with tomato halves, two sardines, followed by thin slices of mozzarella. Drizzle with Bitton Chilli Oil or other chilli oil and reduced balsamic vinegar. Garnish with onion sprouts.

Smoked Salmon with Crab and Celeriac Rémoulade and Green Shallot Dressing

SERVES 4

Rémoulade is a classic French condiment This can be served as a salad dish on its own. It also works as a plate of canapés accompanied by a cocktail or a glass of Champagne. Just serve the green shallot dressing on the side.

200 g celeriac

200 g fresh crabmeat, picked

Juice of 1 lemon

150 g good quality mayonnaise

1 tablespoon dijon mustard

4 tablespoons flat leaf parsley, roughly chopped

Sea salt and white pepper, to season

8 slices (about 145 g) smoked salmon

**8 slices sourdough bread, cut into 4 cm
  squares, toasted**

2 tablespoons salmon roe, to garnish

Chervil sprigs, for garnish

For the green shallot dressing:

**1 bunch of green shallots, green part only,
  washed and trimmed**

¹/₂ cup olive oil

Peel celeriac thickly and rub exposed surfaces with lemon. Grate the celeriac into a bowl, add the crabmeat, lemon juice, mayonnaise, dijon mustard and parsley. Season to taste.

To prepare the green shallot dressing, roughly chop the green shallots and place in a food processor or blender, add the olive oil and process until smooth. Strain and set aside. The dressing can also be poured into a clean jar and stored in the fridge for up to a week.

To serve, place the sourdough toasts on a large serving platter. Lay out the salmon slices on a chopping board and trim into neat rectangles. Place a teaspoon of the rémoulade on the salmon slice about a third of the way down and carefully roll up. Slice into three or four pieces. Stand each roll on a sourdough toast, top with a garnish of salmon roe and a chervil leaf. Drizzle with green shallot dressing.

Bitton

Salad of Chevre, Beetroot, Green Beans and Baby Rocket with Lemon Dressing

SERVES 4

This beautifully coloured salad is easy to put together. You can serve either on its own as an entrée or with some crusty bread for a light lunch. Don't be afraid of cooking fresh beetroot. Once you have tasted beetroot that has been boiled, steamed or roasted you will never go back to the canned version. The star of this dish is the crumbed goat's cheese — the creaminess of the cheese and the crunch of the Japanese breadcrumbs will make you want to make this salad many times over.

600 g fresh beetroot

Preheat oven to 180°C.

For the crumbed goat's cheese:

200 g Panko (Japanese) breadcrumbs

75 g unsalted butter cut into 1 cm cubes

Pinch of sea salt

Pinch of white pepper

150 g chevre (soft goat's curd)

6 tablespoons grapeseed oil for shallow frying

100 g green beans

2 truss tomatoes

200 g rocket, washed, picked

¹/₂ red onion, finely sliced

3 tablespoons Bitton Lemon Dressing or French vinaigrette (see page 174)

Sea salt and white pepper, to season

To prepare the beetroot, cut the tops off the beetroot, leaving at least 2 cm. Scrub the skin, pat dry with paper towels. Wrap each beetroot in foil and place on a baking tray. Cook for 1½ hours until the beetroot is soft.

Unwrap the beetroot and peel when cool enough to handle. Cut the beetroot into wedges, set aside.

For the crumbed goat's cheese, spread the breadcrumbs on a flat tray and place the cubes of butter evenly on the top of the breadcrumbs. Season with salt and white pepper. Place in the oven and bake, stirring occasionally, until the breadcrumbs are lightly toasted (about 8 minutes). Remove and cool.

Slice the goat's cheese into 2 cm thick rounds. Coat the cheese with the breadcrumbs. Place a non-stick frying pan over medium high heat, add the grapeseed oil, heat until the surface shimmers slightly. To test if it is hot enough, place a cube of bread in the pan. If it sizzles, the oil is ready.

continued on page 76

In batches, add the crumbed goat's cheese and fry on each side until golden brown (about 2 minutes each side). Remove, drain on paper towels and set aside.

Drop the beans in boiling water until bright green and just tender. Drain, refresh under cold water. Cut the beans into 4 cm pieces.

In a large bowl, combine the beans, tomato, rocket, onion and beetroot. Add the Bitton Lemon Dressing or French vinaigrette, season to taste. Mix well to evenly coat the salad ingredients with the dressing.

To serve, divide the salad among 4 flat bowls or plates. Place the crumbed goat's cheese on top and serve.

Bitton

CAFÉ

Monday & Tuesday
7am – 5pm

Wednesday to Friday
7am – 9pm

Saturday & Sunday
7am – 5pm

9519 5111

www.bittongourmet.com.au

main course

This is the main event in a traditional French menu — after the entrée comes the main course, salad, then cheese and dessert. My philosophy is that cooking should be as easy as 1,2,3. This means that there are three essential ingredients and three essential components that form the cornerstone for all of my dishes. These three things are the sauce, the meat and the vegetables. Flavours need to be simple, the ingredients fresh and seasonal. You will find that there is a mix of the classics, such as savoury crepes, my signature crispy skin barramundi, all touched with some spice — an influence from Sohani's branch of the family tree. All the recipes give you five-star dining in your own home and can be served as family meals or as part of more elaborate dinner party menus.

Club Sandwich with Chicken, Bacon, Eggs, Tomato, Mayonnaise and Coriander Pesto

SERVES 4

Club sandwiches are said to have originated in a New York gambling club in the late19th century. A maverick line order cook decided that it would be the perfect sustaining snack to bolster patrons and keep them working the tables as long as possible. The owners of the club were pleased and the cook kept his job! The Bitton version of the club sandwich will definitely put you on a winning streak. Fabulous ingredients such as coriander pesto and home-made sauces make this a dish full of flavour and texture for any time of the day — or night.

4 rashers bacon, rind removed

4 eggs, free-range or organic

1 chicken breast, cooked and sliced into
  1 cm slices

2 roma tomatoes, sliced

150 g salad greens, picked, washed and
  dried well

4 tablespoons Bitton Lemon Dressing
  or French vinaigrette (see page 174)

12 slices sourdough bread, toasted

4 tablespoons Bitton Coriander Pesto
  or your favourite herb pesto

150 g mayonnaise (see page 186)

Place a large non-stick frying pan over medium heat. Add the bacon rashers and cook until crispy. Remove and drain on paper towels, set aside. Fry the eggs in the bacon fat until cooked.

Spread mayonnaise on eight slices of the toasted sourdough. Spread four slices of the toasted sourdough with the Bitton Coriander Pesto or your favourite herb pesto.

Place a rasher of bacon and an egg on a pesto-covered slice of toast. Top with a mayonnaise-covered slice of toast, then place chicken, tomato and green salad dressed with Bitton Lemon Dressing or French Vinaigrette on top. Place another mayonnaise-covered slice of toast on top and cut in half to serve.

Peppered Beef Eye Fillet with Pommes Frîtes and Red Wine Sauce

SERVES 4

This dish is the classy French approach to the traditional 'steak and chips'. At Bitton Café, we always serve chips (or pommes frîtes) freshly cut and cooked to order — you can't beat the taste and the crunch. These are spectacular chips and are a perfect accompaniment to the peppered beef or any other dish that needs a side serve of fries, or are great on their own with an ice-cold glass of beer or white wine.

For the peppered beef:

4 x 150 g beef eye fillet

50 g black pepper, coarsely ground

2 tablespoons olive oil

200 ml red wine sauce (see page 194), warmed

Pommes frîtes, to serve (see page 200)

Preheat oven to 180°C (350°F).

Prepare the pommes frîtes and set aside on a warm plate.

For the peppered beef, cover both sides of the beef fillets with black pepper. Place a large frying pan over high heat, add olive oil and heat until smoking. Add beef fillets and sear on both sides. Place the beef fillets on a foil-lined baking tray until cooked to your liking. The way to test your meat is to do the finger to thumb test. Touch your index finger to your thumb and feel the pad of flesh at the base of your fingers — if your meat feels like this, it is rare. Move your middle finger to your thumb; this will give you the feel for medium, third finger to thumb will be well done. Remove from oven and rest in a warm place.

To serve, place the pommes frîtes in the middle of the plate, top with the beef eye fillet and pour a small amount of the red wine sauce over the top. Serve with steamed green beans or a crisp green salad.

Bitton

Croque-Madame Bitton-style with Salad and Spicy Tomato Sauce

SERVES 4

A croque-madame is a croque-monsieur served with a fried egg on top. Basically a croque-monsieur is a grilled ham and cheese sandwich made with emmenthal or gruyère cheese. This dish is a French staple and uses a combination of naughty ingredients — cheese, ham, eggs, toasted bread. My version includes a velvety mornay sauce that makes this dish taste unbelievable. It can be eaten at any time of the day. The addition of a spicy tomato sauce gives the luscious flavours of the sandwich a savoury kick. You can also use your favourite cheese, such as goat's or cheddar.

50 g butter

12 thick slices good quality white bread

6 slices ham

200 ml mornay sauce, (see page 188)

200 g mozzarella, grated

1 tablespoon butter

4 eggs, free-range or organic

For the salad:

100 g salad greens, washed and dried well

2 truss tomatoes, sliced

4 mushrooms, sliced

2 tablespoons Bitton Lemon Dressing
or French vinaigrette (see page 174)

Bitton Spicy Tomato Sauce, to serve

Lay out all the bread slices on a board in rows of three. Butter the bread slices right to the edges. Place the ham on the first and third row of bread. Spread all 12 slices of bread with the mornay sauce and cover with grated cheese. Again, make sure you cover the bread slices right to the very edge, otherwise the edges will dry out. Layer the bread slices on top of each other to make four sandwiches with three tiers — a layer of mornay sauce and cheese, ham in the middle, followed by another layer of mornay sauce and cheese. Cut each stack in half on the diagonal so that you end up with eight 'sandwich' halves. Place on a baking tray and place under a hot grill until golden brown.

In a large non-stick frying pan, melt the butter and fry the eggs. Set aside and keep warm.

Combine the salad ingredients in a small bowl.

To serve, place a 'grilled sandwich' and salad on each serving plate, top with a fried egg. Add a dollop of spicy tomato sauce or tomato relish.

Bitton

Potato Gnocchi with Pumpkin, Tomato Sauce and Mascarpone

SERVES 4

This is Italian comfort food at its best. Gnocchi are delicate little dumplings made out of either potato, semolina or flour. This is a wonderfully filling vegetarian dish that melds the flavours of pumpkin, tomato and mascarpone. Don't be afraid of having a go at making gnocchi. Make sure you work quickly with the gnocchi dough and avoid working it too much so that it doesn't become too heavy.

2 kg desiree potatoes, washed and dried

500 ml milk

200 g semolina

50 g plain flour

2 eggs, beaten

500 g pumpkin, peeled and cut into 2 cm cubes

1 tablespoon olive oil

50 g butter

1 tablespoon garlic, finely chopped

¹/₄ bunch flat leaf (Italian) parsley, finely chopped

700 ml Bitton Spicy Tomato Sauce or your favourite tomato passata spiced up with some chopped chilli

4 tablespoons mascarpone cheese

Preheat oven to 180°C.

Place washed whole potatoes on a baking tray and bake for 1½ to 2 hours until soft or when a skewer is easily inserted into the potatoes. Set aside to cool. When cool enough to handle, peel and place into a large heavy-based saucepan. Mash well (or you can press through a mouli or sieve) so that there are no lumps. Be careful not to over mash as the potatoes will become 'glue-like'.

Toss the pumpkin with the olive oil and place in a baking tray. Bake in the oven for 10 to 15 minutes until the pumpkin is soft and slightly golden on the edges. Remove and set aside.

In a large saucepan, heat the milk and when hot pour into the potato in a thin stream. Mix well with a wooden spoon. Add semolina and flour and continue to stir until the potato mixture is quite stiff and dry, with the liquid being absorbed into the potato.

continued on page 90

Add the eggs and beat well until combined.

To make the gnocchi, take teaspoonfuls of the potato mixture and gently roll into oval shapes. Press the gnocchi onto the tines of a floured fork and place on a chopping board lightly dusted with flour.

Another less messy way of making the gnocchi is to fill a piping bag, hold this over boiling water and squeeze out small dumplings, cutting each little dumpling off with your finger across the piping nozzle.

Fill a large saucepan with water and bring to the boil, salt with about two teaspoons of salt. Once the water boils, drop in small batches of gnocchi. As the gnocchi rises to the top of the boiling water, remove with a slotted spoon and place in a greased baking dish and set aside.

To assemble, place a large frying pan over medium heat and add the butter. When the butter is foaming, add the garlic and cook for a minute. Toss the cooked gnocchi in the pan and cook, stirring gently to coat with the butter and until golden brown. Add the pumpkin, parsley and Bitton Spicy Tomato Sauce or tomato passata. Bring to a simmer.

To serve, spoon into four flat soup bowls and add a dollop of mascarpone. Serve with a crisp green salad.

BITTON
EST 2000
the Bitton room
DAVID Bitton
café
bistro
DAVID Bitton

Wagyu Beef Burger with Pickled Vegetables

SERVES 4

This is classic café fare, the Bitton version of the humble hamburger. The must-have ingredient for this dish is the pickled vegetables, they really shine with the sharp flavour balanced against the rich taste of the wagyu. It is always a sell-out on the menu. This is a juicy and tasty burger that you will never ever get at a drive-thru. Make sure you get hold of good quality pickled vegetables.

4 x wagyu beef burgers (available from good butchers)

100 g button mushrooms, sliced thinly

8 cherry tomatoes, cut in half

3 tablespoons Bitton Lemon Dressing or French vinaigrette (see page 174)

4 x Turkish rolls

4 tablespoons good quality egg mayonnaise

4 tablespoons pickled vegetables of your choice

Preheat oven to 220°C (428°F).

Place a non-stick frying pan over high heat and smear the surface with vegetable oil. Sear the beef burgers on both sides until brown. Remove from pan and place on a lined baking tray and cook in the oven for about 3 minutes or until cooked through.

In a small bowl, place the sliced mushrooms and tomatoes and toss with Bitton Lemon Dressing or French vinaigrette.

Cut the Turkish rolls in half and spread each half with mayonnaise. Add 1 tablespoon of pickled vegetables. Top with beef burger and salad and place the top of the roll. Place each burger on a serving plate alongside a green salad.

Crispy Skin Barramundi with Celeriac Purée and Onion Salsa

SERVES 4

This is the secret to one of my signature dishes. You can use this technique on all types of fish — snapper, salmon, red emperor. Once you perfect it, you will never have plain grilled fish again. The fish is accompanied by one of my favourite vegetables, celeriac. I love celeriac as it reminds me of the wonderful school canteen meals I used to have as a kid. All the food was fresh and seasonal and prepared with some beautiful French sauces.

For the celeriac purée:

2 tablespoons butter

1 onion, finely diced

200 g celeriac, peeled and roughly chopped

500 g potatoes, peeled and roughly chopped

100 g butter

200 ml milk

For the onion salsa:

1/2 brown onion, finely diced

1/2 red onion, finely diced

4 green shallots, finely sliced

1/2 bunch flat leaf parsley, leaves only, chopped

50 ml Bitton Lemon Dressing
  or French vinaigrette (see page 174)

Sea salt and white pepper, to season

Preheat oven to 240°C (460°F).

To make the celeriac purée, place a large saucepan over moderate to high heat. Add butter and onion and sauté for about 3 minutes until slightly softened.

Add the celeriac and potatoes, milk and rest of the butter to the pan, bring to the simmer, cover and cook gently until celeriac and potatoes are soft, about 15 minutes. Drain off excess liquid and purée. Season well and set aside in a warm place.

To make the onion salsa, combine the brown and red onion, green shallots and parsley in a small bowl. Combine the Bitton Lemon Dressing or French vinaigrette, salt and white pepper, pour over the salsa and stir. Set aside until required.

To prepare the barramundi, score the skin of the barramundi with a sharp knife. Using your fingertips, rub the sea salt into the skin.

continued on page 98

Bitton

For the barramundi:

4 (180 g each) barramundi fillets, skin on

Sea salt

1 tablespoon olive oil

Place a large ovenproof frypan over high heat, add olive oil and heat until it begins to smoke. Add the fish, skin side down and press down gently. Cook the fillets for about 3 minutes or until the edges begin to colour. Turn over and cook the other side for 1 minute.

Turn the fillets back to skin-side up, place in oven and bake for 4 minutes or until cooked through and the flesh is firm to the touch.

To serve, place a couple of spoonfuls of celeriac purée onto four plates, top with a large spoonful of onion salsa. Gently place the fish on top of this, skin-side up.

Bitton

Spiced Milk-fed Veal with Kumara Tart, Golden Shallots and Fresh Pea Sauce

SERVES 4

Another classic French dish with the sweetness of the veal spiced up with turmeric. This dish also reflects my philosophy of 1,2,3 — three key ingredients combined simply to great effect — no need for trickery or fancy cooking. A stunning-looking dish for a dinner party.

For the veal:

1 veal loin, weighing approx. 600 g

1 tablespoon turmeric

For the kumara tart:

Good quality puff pastry, such as Carême,
  cut into 4 x 80 mm rounds

350 g kumara (sweet potato), peeled and
  cut into chunks

75 g potato, peeled and cut into chunks

75 g pumpkin, peeled and cut into chunks

50 g butter, diced

80 ml cream

Sea salt and white pepper, to season

For the golden shallots:

50 g butter

40 golden shallots, peeled

1 onion, peeled and finely diced

Preheat oven to 170°C (330°F).

Press the pastry rounds into 4 tart tins. Prick lightly with a fork. Bake the puff pastry according to packet instructions. Set aside to cool.

To prepare the veal loin, place veal in a plastic bag and add the turmeric. Shake the bag until the veal is well coated. Remove from bag and set aside.

To prepare the kumara tarts, place the kumara, potato and pumpkin chunks in a large saucepan. Just cover with water and place over high heat. Bring to the boil, reduce heat and simmer until the vegetables are tender, about 15 minutes. Drain and place in a food processor or blender and purée. Return the purée to the pan and add butter and cream. Mix well until combined. Season with salt and pepper.

To prepare the golden shallot sauce, place a large non-stick frypan over medium heat, melt butter and add golden shallots and onion. Sauté for a few minutes, then add the sugar and stock and bring to the boil.

continued on page 102

Bitton

50 g white sugar

70 ml vegetable stock

1 quantity of fresh pea sauce, (see page 176)

2 teaspoons of red wine sauce (see page 194)

Reduce heat to low, cover with a round of baking paper cut to the same size as the saucepan circumference and cook gently. This will keep the golden shallots submerged in the stock so that they cook evenly. Occasionally remove the greaseproof paper and stir the golden shallots. Cook until tender, about 10 minutes.

To assemble the dish, place a large ovenproof, non-stick frypan over high heat. Seal the veal loin by turning constantly in the pan to keep the meat moist and prevent it from developing a crust. Do this until the turmeric becomes fragrant. Place the veal in the oven and cook for 6 minutes for medium rare, longer for your particular preference. Remove and set aside to rest.

Warm the puff pastry cases in the oven. Place each pastry case in the centre of each serving plate, top with a couple of spoonfuls of the kumara purée. Place three golden shallots around the edge of each kumara tart. Slice the veal into even slices and place on top of the kumara tart. Drizzle the fresh pea sauce around the edge of the plate. Serve immediately.

Moroccan-spiced Lamb with Preserved Lemon Risotto

SERVES 4

This is a fabulous dinner dish. The risotto is a step away from the traditional risotto in that no butter or parmesan is used to finish it. The preserved lemon is what gives the risotto its salty, tangy flavour enhancing the spicy kick of the lamb. Looks glamorous, tastes out of this world and is so simple to put together. Many recipes suggest cooking the rice until it is al dente. I would recommend that you cook the rice to your taste. If you like it, then serve it.

For the preserved lemon risotto:

500 ml veal stock

2 tablespoons olive oil

1 medium brown onion, finely diced

2 garlic cloves, finely diced

200 g arborio rice

250 ml white wine

2 quarters of preserved lemon, rind only,
   finely chopped

For the Moroccan spiced lamb:

4 x 150 g baby lamb rump

1 tablespoon Bitton Moroccan Spice
   or your favourite Harissa spice paste

4 tablespoons olive oil

Sea salt, to season

Preheat oven to 200°C (390°F).

To make the preserved lemon risotto, heat veal stock in a saucepan.

In a heavy-based deep frying pan, add the oil over gentle heat. Add the onion and sauté for a few minutes. Add the garlic and continue cooking until the onion is soft. Add the rice and raise the heat to moderate. Stir to ensure rice is evenly coated with oil and begins to look slightly translucent. Add the wine while continuously stirring the rice and the vegetables.

When the wine is absorbed by the rice, add a ladleful of hot stock. Turn down the heat to a high simmer. Keep adding ladlefuls of stock, stirring and allowing each ladleful to be absorbed before adding the next one. This will take about 20 minutes.

Taste the rice to see if it is cooked. Continue adding the stock until the rice is cooked to your taste. Check the seasoning. Stir through the preserved

continued on page 106

2 tablespoons preserved lemon, finely sliced, to garnish

Small handful of coriander leaves, to garnish

lemon rind and check the seasoning as the preserved lemon can be quite salty. Place the lamb in a bowl with Bitton Moroccan Spice or Harissa paste, and 2 tablespoons of the olive oil. Mix well until the lamb is coated with the spice.

Place a large, ovenproof, non-stick frypan over high heat and add the remaining olive oil. Heat until smoking. Add the lamb and seal well on both sides. Season with salt. Transfer the lamb to the oven and cook through. Generally 8 minutes will give you pink lamb and 16 minutes will give you lamb that is well done. Remove the lamb from the oven and rest for 3 minutes. Carve into thick slices.

To serve, place spoonfuls of risotto on each serving plate and top with slices of lamb. Garnish with preserved lemon and coriander. Lightly steamed beans or a green salad are all that this dish needs as an accompaniment.

Roast Quail Flambé with Fresh Peas

SERVES 4

I have a fondness for quail. Not only does it taste so good, it was a staple of my childhood; my mother served it to the family once a week. It was the meal that we always looked forward to. The quails would be brought to the table in a heatproof dish. My mother would spectacularly flambé the quails with whiskey — we were always entranced by this magic trick and couldn't wait to get stuck in. We would dive in and eat the quails with our fingers, savouring each juicy morsel.

For the peas:

50 g butter

250 g bacon, finely sliced

$^1/_2$ brown onion, finely sliced

2 iceberg lettuce, outer leaves removed, washed and finely sliced

4 spring onions, white part only, finely chopped

1.5 kg fresh green peas, shelled

100 ml chicken stock

1 bouquet garni

2 teaspoons white sugar

Sea salt and white pepper, to season

4 quail, deboned

1 tablespoon olive oil

2 golden shallots, peeled and finely diced

2 tablespoons whiskey

200 ml white wine

To prepare the peas, place a large saucepan over low heat and melt the butter. Add the bacon and onion and sauté until the onion is soft and the bacon has released its fat. Add the lettuce and spring onion, cover and cook slowly for 5 minutes, occasionally stirring the vegetables. Add the peas with the chicken stock, bouquet garni and white sugar. Season to taste with salt and white pepper. Cook for another 10 minutes over low heat until the liquid is reduced by half.

To prepare the quail, place a large, ovenproof frypan or cast-iron casserole dish over medium heat and add the oil. Brown the quail all over — work on 2 minutes each for the breast, underside and the sides of the quail. Add the golden shallots and sauté for a few minutes.

Heat the whiskey and wine in a small saucepan over low heat until just simmering. Light with a long-handled match or lighter and pour over the quail. Cover and transfer to the oven and cook for about 8 to 10 minutes.

To serve, tip the pea and lettuce mixture into casserole dish and rearrange the quail to sit on top.

Orriechetta with Lemon Zest, Basil and Chilli Garlic Masala

This dish is inspired by one I regularly eat at Fratelli Fresh. It is a classic Italian pasta dish that combines the summery tastes of lemon and basil. The addition of chilli garlic masala is perfect with the tomatoes and basil. This is an easy to prepare dish for those times you don't really feel like cooking or you need a quick and healthy meal that will keep your tastebuds and waistline happy. Perfect with a glass of pinot gris or pinot grigio.

750 g orriechetta pasta, dried

125 g butter

1 tablespoon Bitton Chilli Garlic Masala or
 1 tablespoon chilli and garlic, finely chopped

Zest of 1 lemon, finely chopped

200 g cherry tomatoes, halved

8 basil leaves, finely sliced

Sea salt and white pepper, to season

Bring a large pot of water to a rolling boil and add a couple of teaspoons of salt. Add the pasta and stir to prevent them from sticking together. Boil for 8 to 11 minutes, or according to packet instructions. Drain well, stir through a dash of olive oil to prevent the pasta from sticking together and set aside.

Place a large saucepan over medium heat and add the butter. When it is foaming, tip in the cooked pasta and stir to coat with the butter. Add the remaining ingredients and toss gently to combine. Taste for seasoning and serve in pasta bowls.

Casserole of Beef with Vegetables and Pommes Purée

SERVES 6

This is the ideal food for comfort eating over the wintery months. It is a family dish with an earthy flavour that develops through each stage of the cooking process. It is a wonderful example of slow cooking that takes time, although it doesn't necessarily involve constant attention or too much preparation. Allow three days to prepare. This dish tastes great the day after it is made.

250 ml red wine sauce (see page 194)

750 ml cabernet sauvignon

2 medium-sized carrots, peeled and thickly sliced

1.5 kg stewing beef, such as chuck steak or
 gravy beef, cut into golf ball-sized pieces

2 large leeks, washed and white part
 thickly sliced

2 celery sticks, thickly sliced

2 bay leaves

2 sprigs of thyme

1 tablespoon whole black peppercorns

6 small brown onions, peeled

2 tablespoons olive oil

1/2 cup plain flour

3 heaped tablespoons tomato paste

Pommes purée, to serve, (see page 202)

Preheat oven to 220°C (420°F).

Place all the ingredients except olive oil, flour and tomato paste in a large ceramic or glass bowl. Gently mix to combine. Cover with plastic wrap and refrigerate for two days.

Remove the meat from the bowl, drain and pat dry with paper towels. Strain the marinade into a jug and place the vegetables and herbs in a bowl and set aside.

Place a large casserole dish over a medium to high heat. Add olive oil and when it is hot, add the meat in batches, sear on all sides until browned. Remove the meat and set aside in a warm place. Repeat with remaining batches of meat.

Place the reserved vegetables and herbs into the casserole dish. Sauté for 10 to 15 minutes or until the vegetables begin to soften. Return the meat to the casserole dish, sprinkle with plain flour. Stir until well combined.

continued on page 116

Leaving the casserole dish uncovered, place in the oven for 5 minutes. Remove, place on the stove over medium heat. Reduce the oven temperature to 160°C.

Add the reserved marinade to the casserole along with the tomato paste. Stir to combine. Top up with hot water until all the ingredients are just covered. Place the lid on the casserole dish, bring to the boil and place back in the oven for 2 ½ hours.

Serve with pommes purée.

Japanese Pepper Crust Yellowfin Tuna with Braised Tomato and Tamarind Dressing

SERVES 4

When I first came to Australia I was blown away by the Asian flavours that were used in Australian cooking. I had never come across chilli, tamarind, cumin or palm sugar during my time spent cooking in French kitchens. My very formal French approach to food soon became very open-minded; I was prepared to try anything — if it tasted fantastic. This is my nod to Asian cooking using the very best tuna. The tamarind dressing brings a wonderful sweet and sour touch to balance the bite of the Japanese-inspired pepper crust.

For the braised tomato:

9 roma tomatoes

50 g baby carrots, washed, peeled and
  cut into half

50 g butter

50 ml fish stock

1 teaspoon ground cumin

50 g spring onions, cut into 5 cm lengths
  and blanched

For the tamarind dressing:

65 ml tamarind pulp concentrate

340 ml water

90 g palm sugar, shaved

To prepare the braised tomato, peel the tomatoes by cutting a cross in the bottom of them and dropping into boiling water for about 30 seconds. Remove with a slotted spoon, drain and rinse with cold water. The skins will easily slip off the tomatoes. Cut the tomatoes into sixths or eighths lengthways and remove the seeds.

Sauté the carrots in butter until slightly coloured, then slowly add fish stock. When the carrots are nearly cooked through, add the tomato and ground cumin. Add the blanched spring onion and season to taste. Keep warm and set aside until ready to serve.

To prepare the tamarind dressing, soak the tamarind pulp in enough warm water to just cover for about 20 minutes. Remove the pulp and squeeze out any excess liquid. Measure out 65 mls of tamarind water.

continued on page 120

2 cm knob of ginger

300 ml lime juice (about 5 to 6 limes)

100 ml fish sauce

50 ml sesame oil

For the tuna:

4 x 180 g pieces of tuna steaks

1 tablespoon dried chilli flakes

1 tablespoon sesame seeds

1 tablespoon black sesame seeds

1 tablespoon dried oregano, ground

Peel the ginger, chop finely and place in a blender or food processor. Barely cover with water and blend. Strain through a fine sieve.

Combine the tamarind pulp, water and sugar in a small saucepan. Place over low heat and stir until sugar dissolves. Remove from heat and cool. Add the remaining ingredients and stir well to combine.

To prepare the tuna, combine the chilli flakes, sesame seeds and dried oregano on a flat plate. Roll the edges of the tuna steaks in this mixture. Place a large non-stick frypan over medium-high heat and lightly oil the surface. Add the tuna steaks and cook for 2 minutes each side for medium-rare, longer for your preference.

To serve, divide the braised tomatoes among four serving plates, top with a tuna steak and drizzle with the tamarind dressing.

Salmon Braised in a Spicy Tomato Sauce

SERVES 4

This recipe comes from my mother-in-law. My first meal with Sohani's mum saw 'salmon chutney' served. It was made with a spicy sauce and canned pink salmon. My training as a French chef saw to it that I didn't get exposed to exotic spices or food combinations such as chilli and fish. My first taste of spicy food really blew my mind. This is a great hearty meal that can be served up with a rice pilaf or some crusty bread. This is my version of my mother-in-law's dish — she is the cooking matriarch of the family. I have to work hard to impress her.

2 tablespoons olive oil

1 red onion, medium, halved, finely sliced

3 garlic cloves, finely sliced

750 g salmon fillet, skin removed, cut into roughly 2 cm cubes

1 jar Bitton Spicy Tomato Sauce or 500 ml of your favourite tomato passata spiced with some fresh chilli

1 cup coriander, roughly chopped

Preheat oven to 180°C (350°F).

Place a large frying pan over medium heat, add olive oil. Add the onion and sauté until translucent. Add the garlic and chilli (if using). Cook for another 2 to 3 minutes.

Add the salmon pieces to the pan, toss it gently and quickly to seal on all sides.

Add the Spicy Tomato Sauce or tomato passata to the pan and bring to the boil. Allow to simmer, gently turning the salmon pieces until just cooked. This will take about 10 minutes.

Stir in the fresh coriander, remove from the heat and serve immediately with either plain steamed rice or a rice pilaf (see page 206) or plenty of crusty bread to mop up the sauce. A fresh green salad would also be a perfect accompaniment.

Chilli and Garlic Roasted Chicken with Caramelised Vegetables

SERVES 4

My wife Sohani is not known for her culinary talents — that's why she married a chef! This is her signature dish. Every time she serves this, her roast chicken turns out moist and crispy skinned. Served with caramelised vegetables it will turn the traditional Sunday roast into an incredible chicken dish. You can use any type of root vegetables such as carrots, parsnips, potatoes, baby beetroots or swedes.

1 size 16 organic, free-range chicken

1 bulb garlic, skin left on, separated into cloves

3 tablespoons Bitton Chilli Oil or
 good quality chilli oil

Sea salt, to season

1 large red onion, cut into quarters

600 g root vegetables of your choice, peeled,
 cut into 5 cm chunks

1 sprig each of thyme, rosemary, parsley,
 sage, leaves only

Preheat oven to 200°C (390°F).

Rinse the chicken under cold water, pat dry with paper towels. Place all the garlic cloves into the cavity of the chicken. Rub 2 tablespoons of Bitton Chilli Oil or other chilli oil over the skin of the chicken. Season well with sea salt.

Place a large deep non-stick roasting dish over a medium to high heat. Add 1 tablespoon of chilli oil, heat until just smoking. Add the chicken, seal well on all sides for approximately 40 minutes. Work on the basis of sealing the chicken 5 minutes on each side, then 5 minutes on the breast-side of the chicken and another 5 minutes on the back. Remove the chicken, then add the onion, vegetables and herbs to the baking dish. Place the chicken, breast side up, on top of the vegetables. Cook for a further 35 to 40 minutes until the skin is crisp and the chicken is cooked. You can test the 'doneness' by piercing a skewer or knife into the thigh. If the juices run clear, the chicken is cooked.

Remove the chicken, carve and serve, along with the vegetables and onion.

Bitton

Bitton's Famous Moroccan-spiced Chicken Sandwich

SERVES 4

This is a fragrantly spiced version of the regular chicken sandwich. The combination of spices in this dish is a tribute to my grandfather's Moroccan heritage. The zing of the lemon dressing adds an edge to the taste of the spice, complementing the coolness of the yoghurt. A sustaining sandwich that has been a constant on the Bitton Café menu from the beginning. Some regulars will eat it for breakfast, lunch and dinner.

4 medium chicken breast fillets, skin removed

6 tablespoons Bitton Moroccan Spice or
 your favourite harissa or spice paste

1 tablespoon olive oil

100 g mixed lettuce, washed, dried

1 red onion, finely sliced

1 tomato, sliced

Bitton Lemon Dressing or French vinaigrette
 (see page 174), to taste

4 Turkish bread rolls, halved

4 teaspoons natural yoghurt

Preheat the oven to 180°C (350°F).

Place the chicken in a bowl, add 4 tablespoons of Bitton Moroccan Spice or harissa. Mix well to cover and marinate in the fridge for at least 2 hours.

To cook the chicken, place a large non-stick frying pan over a medium heat, add the olive oil. When hot, add the chicken and seal on each side for 2 minutes. Place the chicken on a lightly oiled baking tray and put in the oven for 5 minutes or until cooked. Remove, allow to cool slightly, then cut into 2 cm thick slices.

Place the lettuce, onion and tomato into another bowl, add the Bitton Lemon Dressing or French vinaigrette. Set aside until required.

Spread the remaining Moroccan Spice or harissa evenly over the cut sides of each roll, place in oven and lightly toast the bread, spice side up. Remove, spread the yoghurt on the toasted sides. Distribute the chicken between the rolls, top with salad.

Bitton

Savoury Crêpes with Mushrooms, Spinach and Mornay Sauce

SERVES 4

This is a traditional dish from Brittany. Served alongside a ripe camembert, jam, bread, fresh fruit, a cup of herbal tea and it becomes part of a French/Swiss tradition of a weekly light and simple meal. You can vary the filling by substituting the mushrooms and spinach with cooked prawns or cooked, diced chicken.

For the crêpes:

200 g plain flour

2 free-range or organic eggs, lightly beaten

400 ml milk

100 g butter, melted

extra butter to grease pan

200 ml mornay sauce, (see page 188)

100 g gruyère cheese, grated

500 g button mushrooms, finely sliced

4 bunches English spinach, stems removed, leaves blanched, well drained

Sea salt and white pepper, to season

To make the crêpes, sift the flour into a bowl, make a well in the centre, add the beaten egg and milk. Mix well with a wooden spoon or whisk until well combined and the mixture is smooth. Slowly drizzle in melted butter, stirring to incorporate.

Place a non-stick frypan over medium heat and add a little butter. Pour ¼ of a cup of the crêpe mixture into the hot pan, swirling the mixture to completely coat the base of the pan. When the edges start to brown, carefully flip the crêpe over to brown the other side. Slide onto a plate and continue with the rest of the crêpe mixture.

To serve, place the crêpes on a clean, dry surface, such as a large chopping board, spread with a couple of tablespoons of mornay sauce, sprinkle with half the grated cheese. Top the crêpes with the sliced mushrooms and drained spinach, season and roll up. Place the filled crêpes in a greased baking tray, cover with the remaining mornay sauce and sprinkle with the rest of the cheese. Place under a hot grill to melt the cheese until golden.

dessert

The word 'dessert' comes from the Old French

desservir, literally translated as 'to clear the table' and 'to serve'. To me, this means that dessert must be a knockout to really end the meal on a high. Simplicity, as always, is the key. There are some old-school favourites such as Gaby's sticky date pudding (that we can never take off the menu), bread and butter pudding and a hot chocolate fudge cake. You can also dip into desserts that will become part of your own family tradition — apple tart, crème caramel, French crepes with vanilla bean ice cream and orange jelly. Some of the desserts are ones where I've combined the French culinary classics with some of my own experiments that have produced strawberry, lime and basil mousse, exotic fruit salad with lemongrass broth and a luscious baked mango and ginger cheesecake. The only difficulty with these recipes is choosing which one to make!

Dessert

Strawberry, Lime and Basil Mousse

SERVES 6

Strawberry, lime and basil are made for each other. The clean, grassy flavour of the basil cuts through the sweetness of the strawberries and the lime lifts this mousse into the realm of the angels. It is a perfect dessert to serve on a hot summer night. This dessert can also be served in individual dishes.

80 g caster sugar

$^{1}/_{2}$ cup basil, finely chopped

5 g powdered gelatine

150 ml lime juice (about 3 to 4 limes)

375 ml cream

375 g strawberries, washed, hulled, sliced

1 layer of sponge cake, cut to fit the base
 of terrine/loaf tin

150 g Bitton Strawberry and Vanilla Jam

A few extra basil leaves, finely shredded,
 to serve

Place a small saucepan over a low heat, add the sugar along with 4 ½ tablespoons of water. Stir until the sugar dissolves. Increase the heat and bring to the boil. Remove the sugar syrup from the heat, add the basil and set aside to cool.

Place the gelatine in a bowl, add 1½ tablespoons of boiling water. Stir until the gelatine dissolves. Add the lime juice, then combine with the cooled basil and sugar syrup. Beat the cream until soft peaks form and fold into the basil mixture. Line a terrine or loaf tin with plastic wrap, bringing it up over the sides of the tin. Place a layer of sliced strawberries to cover the base of the tin. Pour in the basil and cream mixture, smooth the top. Shake the tin slightly to dispel any air bubbles. Top with another layer of sliced strawberries.

Gently place the sponge cake on the strawberries. Fold over excess plastic wrap and refrigerate for 4 hours or until set.

To serve, dip the terrine very briefly into warm water and turn out onto a flat plate. With a sharp knife dipped in hot water, slice the terrine into even slices. Place each slice on a serving plate. Combine the remaining strawberries, basil, Strawberry and Vanilla Jam or other strawberry jam and serve alongside the mousse.

Vanilla and Coffee Crème Brûlée

SERVES 6

This is a classic petits fours that was served during my time as head chef at Gekko, Sheraton on the Park. It is easy to do, looks great, making it a dinner party staple. If possible, get hold of a small kitchen gas blowtorch (these are available at most kitchen shops) to caramelise the sugar on top of the brûlées. You need a hard shell of caramel to hide the silkiness of the custard underneath. The coffee is a great flavour for this dish. Be a little adventurous and experiment with other flavours, such as citrus zest, rosewater or spices such as cardamom, cinnamon or nutmeg.

300 ml cream

200 ml full-cream milk

$^1/_2$ vanilla bean

$^1/_4$ cup coffee beans

6 free-range or organic egg yolks

100 g sugar

For the caramel topping

6 teaspoons demerara sugar

Preheat oven to 90°C (190°F).

In a medium-sized saucepan, bring the cream, milk, vanilla bean and coffee beans to a simmer over low heat. Remove from heat. In a separate bowl, whisk together the egg yolks and sugar until the sugar is dissolved and the mixture is pale and thick. Strain the hot milk mixture into the egg mixture, whisking all the time, until the mixture thickens. Pour into six 200 ml ramekins. Place in a baking dish lined with a tea towel (this will stop custards from getting too hot at the base of the dish), fill the baking dish with hot water to come three-quarters of the way up the side of the ramekins. Cook for 45 minutes.

When the custards are cooked, (you can gauge this by inserting a sharp knife and if it comes out clean, it is ready). Remove from oven, cover and chill for at least 2 hours. Sprinkle a teaspoon of demerara sugar over each custard and heat with a gas blowtorch for a few minutes until the sugar caramelises.

Bitton

Hot Chocolate Fudge Cake

SERVES 8

This is my daughter Monet's favourite and I wouldn't dare not include this. It is the perfect chocolate cake to serve for dessert or even a decadent afternoon tea, or for satisfying chocolate cravings at any time of the day. This recipe is also deceptively simple resulting in an intense chocolate flavour, a more-ish cake with a soft 'fudgy' centre. Add some finely grated orange zest to the mixture for a more 'grown-up' chocolate cake. Serve with a berry coulis and vanilla bean ice cream. Fresh raspberries are a great accompaniment, too.

$^1/_2$ **cup cocoa powder**

1 $^1/_2$ **cups self-raising flour**

1 tablespoon bicarbonate of soda (baking soda)

$^1/_2$ **cup caster sugar**

250 g good quality chocolate,
 broken into small pieces

80 g butter

3 free-range or organic eggs

200 g condensed milk

1 cup plain yoghurt

For the mixed berry coulis:

$^1/_2$ **punnet each of strawberries, blueberries,**
 raspberries (frozen can also be used)

3 teaspoons of icing sugar, sifted

Good quality vanilla bean ice cream, to serve

Preheat the oven to 170°C (330°F). Grease 8 soufflé or dariole moulds. This can also be made as a 26 cm round cake.

Into a large bowl, sift all the dry ingredients. Mix to combine.

In a double saucepan or a bowl placed over a saucepan of simmering water, gently melt the chocolate and butter. Stir until combined and glossy. Cool slightly. Add eggs, condensed milk and yoghurt to the chocolate mixture. Stir well to combine.

Make a well in the dry ingredients, gradually pour in the chocolate/egg mixture, stirring continuously. Pour into the prepared moulds and cook for 20 minutes until the top of the cake is firm to the touch. The inside of the cake should be slightly gooey.

To prepare the mixed berry coulis, place the berries in a food processor or blender. Add the sifted icing sugar, blend until smooth. Strain through a sieve.

Turn out onto serving plates. Serve with mixed berry coulis and a scoop of vanilla bean ice cream.

Bitton

French Crêpes with Vanilla Bean Ice Cream and Orange Jelly

SERVES 4 TO 6

The origin of Bitton Orange Jelly is a beautiful mistake. The original recipe was for marmalade. However, it was one that didn't turn out the way it was supposed to. It did end up as an orange jelly with the luscious undertones of toffee. The caramelised orange jelly turns simple crêpes into a decadent brunch or an elegant dessert dish.

200 g plain flour

Pinch of salt

30 g castor sugar

3 medium free-range or organic eggs,
 lightly beaten

50 g butter, melted with solids removed

250 ml milk

Butter for frying

500 ml good quality vanilla bean ice cream

4 tablespoons of Bitton Orange Jelly
 or maple syrup or honey

For the crêpes, sift the flour, salt and sugar into a mixing bowl. Make a well in the centre of the mixture, add the eggs. Using a whisk, gradually bring the dry mixture into the eggs, followed by the milk, then the melted butter. Whisk gently until the mixture is smooth, being careful not to over-mix.

Place a large non-stick frying pan over a medium heat, add ½ teaspoon butter. Add a spoonful of the crêpe mixture to the middle of the pan, swirl to cover the base of the pan. When the edges of the crêpes turn brown, gently turn them over with a spatula (unless you feel confident you can flip them by tossing the pan up and down). Cook until golden. Turn out onto a warmed plate, fold in half, then quarters, stack and serve with a generous scoop of vanilla bean ice cream and a tablespoon of Orange Jelly or maple syrup or honey drizzled over the top.

Little Chocolate Friands with Candied Orange

MAKES 30

These little cakes are moist, dense and almondy mouthfuls, flavoured with a touch of cocoa. A natural partner with a shot of espresso or maybe a couple to accompany a latte. The flavourings can be changed to include lemon zest and poppy seeds, swirls of pureed raspberry or finely diced apple.

6 free-range or organic egg whites

$^1/_2$ cup icing sugar, sifted

$^1/_2$ cup rice flour

1 vanilla bean, split and seeds scraped

1 cup almond meal

1 tablespoon cocoa powder, sifted

150 g butter, melted and cooled slightly

For the candied orange:

1 orange, washed, the zest removed
  in a long strip

375 ml water

340 g caster sugar

Soak zest in cold water for two hours. Remove and dry well. Julienne. Blanch zest in 500 ml boiling water for 30 seconds. Repeat the blanching/boiling process three times. Drain and set aside.

Place a small saucepan over high heat. Add the water and caster sugar, and bring to the boil. Add the blanched orange zest to the sugar syrup and simmer over low heat until the liquid disappears. Make sure the sugar syrup does not caramelise. Remove and place on a wire rack to dry.

For the friands:

Preheat the oven to 170 °C and grease 3 x 12 mould mini muffin tins.

In a large bowl, lightly whisk the egg whites until frothy and add the icing sugar, rice flour, vanilla bean seeds, almond meal and cocoa powder. Add the melted butter to the egg white mixture in a thin stream, stirring gently to incorporate. Fill the muffin tins no more than two-thirds full and cook for 10 to 15 minutes until firm to the touch. Remove from oven and cool in tins for 5 minutes. Carefully turn out onto wire racks to cool completely. Garnish each friand with some candied orange.

Bitton

Bread and Butter Pudding with Crème Anglaise

SERVES 6

This is a traditional British pudding that has evolved from the 17th century 'bread pudding', a way of using up stale bread. During the 1980s and 1990s the classic bread and butter pudding was again on the menu, this time with more exotic ingredients. This is the Bitton version with the addition of a rich vanilla custard. Use the best ingredients — eggs, milk, vanilla — for a wonderfully simple dessert.

For the bread and butter pudding:

500 g day-old bread (you can use any type of bread, brioche or croissants)

5 free-range or organic eggs

3 free-range or organic egg yolks

1 litre full-cream milk

175 g caster sugar

1 vanilla bean, split in half

2 tablespoons brown or demerara sugar

For the crème anglaise:

500 ml full-cream milk

6 free-range or organic egg yolks

250 g caster sugar

1 vanilla bean

Preheat the oven to 150°C (300°F).

Grease a 25 cm ovenproof dish — a size to fit all the bread slices in one layer.

For the bread and butter pudding, slice the bread into 2 cm slices. Place on the base of the prepared dish.

Lightly whisk the eggs, egg yolks, milk and sugar in a large jug. Scrape the seeds from the vanilla bean, stir into the mixture.

Pour about three-quarters of the egg/milk mixture over the bread layer. Let it sit for 5 minutes allowing the mixture to soak into the bread before adding the rest of the mixture.

Evenly sprinkle the sugar over the top of the dish. Bake for 35 to 40 minutes until set. The top of the custard will be slightly firm to the touch.

continued on page 148

For the crème anglaise, in a medium-sized saucepan, bring the milk with the vanilla bean to a simmer over low heat. Remove from heat, take out the vanilla bean and split it in half. In a separate bowl, whisk together the egg yolks, sugar and scraped out seeds of the vanilla bean until pale and thick.

Strain the hot milk onto the egg mixture, whisking all the time, until the mixture thickens. Pour back into the saucepan, return to stove over low heat. Using a wooden spoon, continually stir the custard until it begins to thicken, coating the back of the spoon. This can take about 10 minutes or more. Remove from the heat and cool.

To serve, cut the bread and butter pudding into squares. Place on serving plates. Spoon over crème anglaise. For a decadent treat, add a scoop of vanilla bean ice cream.

Gaby's Sticky Date Pudding with Caramel Sauce

SERVES 6

This well-known dessert has been around since the mid 1990s when it really took Australia by storm. Every restaurant and café served it. It combines a sweet sponge base with a rich caramel sauce. Gaby is our business partner, working with Bitton since the very first day. This is his take on this much-loved favourite — a light date sponge topped with a divine sticky sauce. Leftover sauce can be kept in the fridge to be reheated as a delicious hot sauce for ice cream.

For the pudding:

250 g pitted dates, roughly chopped

450 ml water

1 tablespoon bicarbonate of soda (baking soda)

160 g butter

250 g caster sugar

3 free-range or organic eggs

250 g plain flour, sifted

For the caramel sauce:

250 ml cream

125 g brown sugar

50 g butter

Vanilla bean ice cream, to serve

Preheat oven to 180°C (350°F). Grease six ovenproof ramekins or line a six-hole muffin tin with baking paper.

For the pudding, place the dates with the water in a small saucepan over medium heat, bring to the boil. Remove from heat, stir in the bicarbonate of soda. Cream butter and sugar, add eggs, one at a time, beating well after each addition. Gently fold in the flour, stir in the dates with their liquid, pour the mixture into the tin/moulds. Cook for 45 minutes or until the top of the pudding springs back when lightly touched.

For the caramel sauce, melt the brown sugar and butter in a saucepan over low heat. Stir until combined and the sugar has dissolved. Add the cream slowly, stirring gently. Bring the sauce to the boil. Simmer for 5 minutes.

To serve, unmould the puddings. Pour the sauce over the top. Serve while still warm with vanilla bean ice cream.

Apple Tart

SERVES 8

This is a wonderful dessert — apples, puff pastry, cream. It looks beautiful on the plate; a classy finish to any meal.

375 g good quality puff pastry,
 such as Carême
350 g granny smith apples, peeled
 and quartered
25 ml water
25 g caster sugar
1 vanilla bean, split in half

250 g granny smith apples
30 g butter, melted
100 g apricot jam, warmed, for glazing

Mascarpone cheese or cream, to serve

Preheat oven to 250°C (480°F). Roll out the pastry, then cut eight 10 cm rounds of pastry. Place on a baking tray lined with baking paper. With a sharp knife, lightly score a border about a ½ cm in from the edge of the pastry. This will form the sides of each tart. Prick all over with a fork.

Rest the pastry cases in the fridge while you prepare the apples. Place 350 g apples in a large saucepan over low heat. Sprinkle the sugar over the apples and add the vanilla bean. Cook slowly for 10 to 15 minutes until the apples are soft, pulpy, and the excess liquid has evaporated. Remove from heat and cool. Push the apples through a fine mesh sieve. Set aside.

Peel and core the rest of the apples. Slice into paper-thin slices.

Remove the chilled pastry cases and fill the inner circle with the apple purée. Top the purée with the sliced apple, starting at the centre of the tart, forming concentric circles of apple out to the edge of the pastry. Brush melted butter around the edge of the pastry. Place the tarts in the oven. Bake for 10 minutes. Reduce the heat to 180°C (350°F). Cook for another 6 or 7 minutes until the pastry is golden brown and the apple slices slightly caramelised.

Remove the tarts, brush the top with the jam glaze. Serve with a spoonful of mascarpone or cream.

Crème Caramel

This was one of the first dishes I learnt to cook when I began my apprenticeship in 1984. I remember clearly how the making of the caramel terrified me as I didn't want to burn it, ruining the dish. Over the years I've overcome my fear; practice makes perfect. This is a French classic that no dinner party should be without.

For the caramel:

50 ml water

150 g caster sugar

For the crème:

3 free-range or organic eggs

500 ml full-cream milk

100 g sugar

1 vanilla bean, split in half

Preheat oven to 90°C (190°F).

Lightly grease a large round baking dish or ten small dariole moulds or soufflé dishes.

To make the caramel, combine the sugar and water in a small saucepan over gentle heat. Stir until sugar dissolves. Increase the heat to medium, bringing the syrup to the boil without stirring. Cook until mixture turns a dark caramel colour, this will take about 10 minutes. Immediately pour into the prepared dishes as this will stop the caramel cooking further.

To make the custard, lightly whisk the eggs, milk and sugar. Scrape in vanilla seeds, strain and pour into the caramel-lined dishes. Place in a baking dish lined with a tea towel (this will stop the custards from getting too hot at the base of the dish), pour in enough water to come just over halfway up the sides. Bake for an hour until just set. Remove the custards, cool, then place in refrigerator overnight.

To serve, using your fingertips, gently press the top edges of the crème caramels to release them. Carefully invert onto serving plates.

RESERVED

46 4

Bitton's Tiramisu

SERVES 6

Tiramisu is Italian for 'pick-me-up'. A dessert made of coffee-soaked biscuits covered in rich custard cream. It is also my way of showing the Italians that the French can do this with style. This is a quick and easy dish that has everything to make a delectable dessert — coffee, cream, biscuits. The grated chocolate and strawberries are literally the icing on the cake. This has been a constant on the Bitton Café menu.

80 g pure icing sugar

3 free-range or organic egg yolks

250 g mascarpone cheese

1 free-range or organic egg white

4 tablespoons powdered chocolate

2 teaspoons warm water

$1/2$ to $1/4$ cup strong black coffee
  or espresso, cooled plus extra for drizzling

12 savoiardi (sponge) biscuits,
  cut in half crossways

6 teaspoons each of powdered chocolate and
  sifted icing sugar, to serve

Beat together the icing sugar and egg yolks until thick and pale. Fold in mascarpone until mixed through. In a separate bowl, whip the egg white until soft peaks form, then fold into the mascarpone mixture. Set aside.

In a small bowl, combine powdered chocolate and warm water to create a 'chocolate' sauce. Drizzle this on the inside of the serving glasses.

Pour the cooled coffee or espresso into a shallow dish. Soak each savoiardi biscuit in the coffee. Place biscuits in the bottom of six latte glasses. Top with mascarpone mixture, filling up two-thirds of the glass. Add more soaked biscuits, followed by the rest of the mascarpone mixture. Smooth the top and place in the fridge to set for a minimum of 1 hour.

To serve, sprinkle the tops of the tiramisus, half with powdered chocolate and the other half with sifted icing sugar.

Baked Mango and Ginger Cheesecake

SERVES 8

This is an upmarket cheesecake with a nod to the New York cheesecake and its sour cream topping. A baked cheesecake has more substance and texture than some of the light and fluffy store-bought ones. The addition of mango and ginger lifts this cheesecake, reminding you that life is too short to eat a bad cheesecake. Enjoy.

For the biscuit base:

260 g digestive biscuits

40 g desiccated coconut

100g butter, melted

For the cheesecake:

500 g cream cheese

200 g caster sugar

4 free-range or organic eggs

2 tablespoons lemon juice

2 drops pure vanilla essence

400 ml sour cream

3 heaped tablespoons Bitton Mango and Ginger Jam or a good quality apricot jam

1 large mango or apricots, thinly sliced, to garnish

Grease and line a 20cm round springform pan. In a food processer, place the biscuits, desiccated coconut and process until the mixture resembles fine breadcrumbs. Add the butter and process again until well combined. Spoon the biscuit mix into the pan. Using the base of a glass tumbler press out to cover the base of the pan evenly. Refrigerate for 30 minutes.

Preheat the oven to 180°C (350°F).

Place the cream cheese and caster sugar into a food processor and process until smooth. Add the eggs, one at a time, followed by the lemon juice and vanilla essence. Process again until well combined. Pour the cream cheese mixture on top of the biscuit base. Place in the oven. Bake for 45 minutes or until just firm to the touch.

In a mixing bowl, place the sour cream and Bitton Mango and Ginger Jam or apricot jam and stir until well combined. Pour the mixture over the top of the baked cheesecake and return to the oven for a further 10 minutes. Remove and allow to cool. Refrigerate overnight until set.

To decorate, place mango or apricot slices on top of the cheesecake.

Exotic Fruit Salad with Lemongrass Broth and Ginger Ice Cream

SERVES 8

This is a spectacular dessert that takes advantage of the abundance of exotic fruit available in Australia. You can use any combination of fruit such as kiwifruit, blueberries and raspberries. It is a perfect ending to a summer evening meal.

For the lemongrass broth:

200 ml water

200 ml caster sugar

1 stick lemongrass, 20 cm white part,
  slightly bruised with the back of a knife.

For the fruit salad:

4 tamarillos, peeled, quartered

2 mangoes, peeled, sliced

2 dragonfruit, peeled, sliced

2 starfruit, washed, sliced

Good quality ginger ice cream, to serve

In a small saucepan, over medium heat, combine the sugar, water and lemongrass. Bring to the boil, reduce the heat, simmer for 10 minutes. Strain and chill in the refrigerator.

Combine the fruit in a serving bowl. Pour the chilled lemongrass broth over the top. Serve with ginger ice cream.

Bitton

Poached Pear with Gratinated Blue Cheese and Cayenne Pepper

SERVES 4

A French meal is always finished with a cheese course — a perfectly ripe cheese, served with fresh seasonal fruit. When I was growing up, my family grew most of their fruit and vegetables. I remember being involved at harvest time picking the fruit from the 15 pear trees, 80 apple trees and five cherry trees. Pears are one of my favourite fruits (I've been an ambassador for the Australian Pear Industry since 2008). This dessert is my way of combining blue cheese and sweet corella pears. A little unusual but a wonderful and easy-to-prepare dessert.

400 ml water

200 g sugar

5 star anise

2 cloves

1 cinnamon quill

2 cardamom pods

2 corella pears, ripe not soft

100 g soft blue cheese, such as **Milawa Blue**

100 ml cream

1/2 teaspoon cayenne pepper

20 g pine nuts, lightly toasted

For the poaching liquid, combine the water, sugar and spices in a large saucepan. Place over medium heat. Bring to the boil, then reduce to a simmer.

Peel the pears, then lower the pears into the simmering syrup, cook until tender, about 10 to 15 minutes. Remove the pears, place on a wire rack to cool. Reserve 100 ml of the poaching liquid.

Halve the pears, scoop out the core with a melon baller or teaspoon, leaving a little hollow in each pear half. Fill with a tablespoon of blue cheese. Place in an ovenproof serving dish, put under a hot grill until the cheese begins to melt.

For the cayenne sauce, bring the remaining poaching liquid to the boil, add the cream and the cayenne pepper. Cook for 5 minutes. Remove from heat.

To serve, pour the cayenne cream sauce over the pears, sprinkle with toasted pine nuts.

the Bitton room

DAVID
Bitton

sauces and sides

French sauces date back to the Middle Ages and were slowly refined to become the foundation on which French cuisine has developed. During the 18th century Marie Antoine Carême was the founder of classic French cuisine and was responsible for recording and creating a framework from which all French cooking now comes from. A hundred years later, Georges Auguste Escoffier revised and modernised cooking in France. As part of my apprenticeship I had to learn how to make every type of sauce out of the classic Escoffier book. The sauces are not only used as toppings for various foods but they are often included as part of the ingredients list to add an extra dimension to the dish.

Aside from the history, the following sauces are wonderful to have in your repertoire as they can be used for many dishes and the variations on flavourings are never-ending. These sauces will definitely add a five-star touch for the meals you prepare for your family and friends.

I have also included some of my favourite side dishes, from the well-known Pommes Frîtes (also known around the world as French fries) to the much-loved Pommes Purée (or potato mash done the French way). The Rice Pilaf is a great addition to curries and seafood, or wherever you feel the need to serve rice with a bit of spice.

Sauces and sides

Buerre Blanc

Buerre Blanc literally translates as white butter. This is a rich, hot butter sauce that is made with a reduction of white wine and vinegar or lemon juice. It is a wonderful sauce to serve with fish, poached eggs or steamed potatoes. The sauce is incredibly versatile. Its use is only limited by your imagination.

100 ml white wine

2 bay leaves

5 white peppercorns

$^1/_2$ onion, finely diced

200 ml cream

250 g butter, diced

$4^1/_2$ tablespoons lemon juice

Sea salt and white pepper, to season

Place a small saucepan over medium heat. Add white wine, bay leaves, white peppercorns, onion and cream, bring to a simmer, reduce the liquid by half. Strain. Drop the heat to low and return liquid to pan. Add the butter to the wine mixture, dropping in a few cubes of butter at a time while continuously stirring with a wooden spoon. When all the butter is incorporated, add lemon juice and season to taste.

French Vinaigrette

Salad is a key component of French meals. Naturally it should be given a substantial and delicious dressing to help complete the meal. No self-respecting Frenchman would turn down a salad.

50 g golden shallots, finely diced

200 ml red wine vinegar

1 free-range or organic egg yolk

400 ml vegetable oil

1 teaspoon dijon mustard

Sea salt and white pepper, to season

In a clean bowl, marinate the diced golden shallots in the red wine vinegar for 15 minutes. Add the rest of the ingredients, except for the salt and white pepper, whisk to combine. Season, set aside. Store in a clean glass jar or bottle in the fridge.

Fresh Pea Sauce

When fresh green peas are in season use this sauce to your culinary advantage. It is a stylish accompaniment to any delicate meat, such as veal or chicken or lamb. See the Spiced Milk-fed Veal with Kumara Tart on page 100. It will also add a depth to simple vegetable dishes.

50 g butter

1 onion, finely diced

400 g fresh peas, shelled, blanched

500 ml litre cream

25 g baby spinach, washed, dried well

Sea salt and white pepper, to season

Place a large saucepan over medium heat. Melt the butter. Add the onion, sauté until soft and translucent. Add the blanched peas and warm through. Add the cream, bring the mixture to the boil. Add the baby spinach, cook until wilted. Remove from heat, blend in a food processor and pour the sauce through a fine strainer into a large jug. Season to taste, cover and keep warm.

Green Peppercorn Sauce

A French classic! Serve with a perfectly grilled steak and pommes frîtes for an elegant 'pub meal' at home. After you have cooked your meat, use the same frypan tto make the sauce. The meat juices will add a wonderful flavour.

50 g butter

1 onion, finely diced

1 teaspoon garlic, finely chopped

100 g green peppercorns

300 ml red wine sauce (see page 194)

500 ml cream

Sea salt and white pepper, to season

Place a saucepan over low heat. Melt the butter, add the onion and garlic, sauté for 5 minutes. Add the green peppercorns, cook for another 5 minutes. Add the red wine sauce and cream, simmer gently, reducing the liquid by half. Season to taste. The sauce can be strained through a sieve or served with the peppercorns.

Hollandaise Sauce

This is an emulsion of egg yolk and butter seasoned with lemon juice. It is also rich, buttery and is the undisputed partner of poached egg and asparagus. The hollandaise sauce is one that needs respect and care. Don't be afraid of making it — feel the fear and make it anyway. With this recipe you can't go wrong. If the sauce splits add a tiny amount of warm water and continue mixing to amalgamate the mixture. Or repeat the whisking of the egg yolks over simmering water, add the split sauce and re-whisk again until smooth.

4 free-range or organic egg yolks

1 tablespoon white wine vinegar

1 tablespoon cold water (approx.), measure out by ladling in the water in 3 half eggshells

100 ml clarified butter, melted, cooled slightly

1 tablespoon lemon juice

Sea salt and white pepper, to season

Place the egg yolks in a very clean and dry stainless steel bowl. Keeping the bowl clean and dry preserves the integrity of the sauce, keeping the flavour of the sauce untainted. Suspend the bowl over a saucepan of cold water. The base of the bowl should not touch the water. Add the vinegar and the water. Place the pan over a moderate heat, whisk this mixture until the water comes to a boil, then reduce the heat to a steady simmer. Whisk until the mixture becomes thick and foamy. Remove the bowl from the heat. Set aside for 1 or 2 minutes. Add the clarified butter in a slow, steady stream. Continue whisking until all the butter is incorporated and the sauce is smooth and glossy. Stir through the lemon juice. Season to taste with salt and white pepper. Remove from heat and keep warm.

To make a mousseline sauce, allow the hollandaise sauce to cool to barely warm. Whip 50 ml of fresh cream to the same consistency as the hollandaise sauce and gently fold into the sauce.

This sauce is delicious with artichokes, prawns and crabmeat.

Marie Rose Sauce

Marie Rose sauce is the sauce that is commonly served with a prawn cocktail. Try it with any other type of seafood such as lobster tails, Balmain bugs, yabbies or lightly poached white fish. Also delicious stirred through cooked potatoes for a different take on the standard potato salad. Serve with cold roasted meats and it creates another wonderful combination of flavours.

100 ml good quality mayonnaise

2 teaspoons cognac

Sea salt and white pepper, to season

Pinch of ground cayenne pepper

2 teaspoons tomato sauce (ketchup)

Juice of 1 lemon

In a small bowl combine all the ingredients, mixing to a smooth sauce. Cover and place in the refrigerator until ready to serve.

Mayonnaise

There are some great commercial mayonnaises available on the market, however, you can't beat the flavour of home-made mayonnaise. You need a little bit of patience and elbow grease to blend the oil and the egg yolks.

5 free-range or organic egg yolks

1 tablespoon white wine vinegar

2 tablespoons Dijon mustard

Pinch each of sea salt and white pepper

500 ml vegetable or olive oil

Place a clean bowl on a folded tea towel on your bench top.

Whisk together the egg yolks, vinegar and mustard. Add salt and white pepper. Continue whisking while adding the oil, drop by drop into the egg mixture, slowly increasing to a very slow stream, until incorporated and the mayonnaise is thick. This could take up to 10 minutes.

Check seasoning before using the mayonnaise.

Mornay Sauce

This is basically a béchamel sauce flavoured with cheese. It is great for using in all types of dishes from filling crépes, to cauliflower cheese or blanketing any type of vegetable.

1 litre milk

100 g clarified butter

100 g plain flour

Pinch of freshly grated nutmeg

100g gruyère cheese, grated

1 free-range or organic egg yolk

To make the mornay sauce, place the milk in a large heavy-based saucepan over medium heat. Bring to boil, reduce heat and simmer. In a small saucepan placed over medium heat, melt the butter, then whisk in the flour, stirring continuously for 5 minutes. Add the butter mixture to the hot milk, continue to whisk until the sauce thickens and coats the back of a spoon. Add nutmeg. Stir through the grated cheese and the egg yolk. Set aside and cool slightly before using.

Reduced Balsamic Vinegar

This is a sweet-sour sauce that goes well drizzled over bitter salad leaves, seafood such as scallops or lightly grilled prawns. The reduction of the balsamic vinegar really heightens the flavour.

1 cup of good quality balsamic vinegar

Place the balsamic vinegar in a small saucepan over medium heat. Bring to the boil, then reduce heat to low. Simmer until 1 tablespoon of thick syrup is left in the saucepan.

Red Wine Sauce

A rich and delicious sauce that blends the sweetness and fragrance of herbs and vegetables with the deep flavour of red wine. A great accompaniment to any meat dish.

2 tablespoons olive oil

300 g beef trimmings

2 carrots, peeled and finely diced

1 onion, peeled and finely diced

4 sticks of celery, finely diced

2 cloves of garlic, finely chopped

$1/2$ bunch of thyme

2 bay leaves

1 tablespoon tomato puree (passata)

150 ml sherry vinegar

$1/2$ cup sugar

150 ml port

500 ml red wine

3 litres of good quality veal stock

Place a large deep-sided frypan over medium heat. Add olive oil and sauté the beef trimmings until dark brown and well caramelised. Add the diced carrots, onion, celery, garlic, thyme and bay leaves and cook for a further 3 minutes. Add the tomato passata and cook for another 10 minutes, stirring occasionally, until the mixture is sticky. Add the sherry vinegar and sugar and bring to the boil. Cook for 5 minutes. Add the port, bring back to the boil and reduce the sauce by half (this should take about 5 to 8 minutes. Add the red wine and stock and reduce by half again (this should take about an hour). Strain through a sieve lined with muslin cloth into another large saucepan. Place the pan over medium heat and bring to the boil. Reduce again until the sauce is thick and coats the back of a spoon.

Pommes de terre Dauphinoise

SERVES 4

This is a gorgeous way of serving potatoes. Layers of potatoes and golden cheese makes this a comforting yet impressive side dish.

350 ml milk

350 ml cream

1 large garlic clove, sliced

1 sprig thyme

1 bay leaf

Sea salt and white pepper, to season

600 g desiree potatoes, washed

4 free-range or organic egg yolks

90 g gruyère cheese

Preheat the oven to 180° C

Peel and cut the potatoes into approximately $\frac{1}{2}$ cm thick slices.

Place a large heavy-based saucepan over medium heat. Add the milk and cream, bringing to the boil. Add the garlic, herbs and seasoning and allow to simmer for 2 to 3 minutes. Gently place the potato slices into the milk-cream mixture and cook for 5 to 6 minutes or until just tender. Drain the potato slices, reserving the liquid.

Allow the liquid to cool slightly, then carefully mix in the egg yolks.

On a lined baking tray, place a single layer of potato and top with grated gruyère cheese. Drizzle with a little of the reserved liquid. Repeat until all the potato has been used up. Sprinkle the remaining cheese over the top of the potato layers. Place in the oven for 15 minutes or until just brown and bubbling around the edges. Cut into portions with a sharp knife and serve.

Pommes Frîtes

Classic French fries. Once you eat handmade chips you will never go back to tipping them out of a plastic packet again. Serve this potato dish with anything — these are rockstar chips.

800 g desirée potatoes, peeled,
cut into wedges
Oil for deep frying
Sea salt, to season

Place a large, heavy frying pan over high heat. Pour in the oil and heat until bubbling slightly. To test if the oil is hot enough, drop in a small cube of bread; if it sizzles then the oil is ready. Add the potato wedges in 2 to 3 batches until golden brown and cooked through. This will take about 5 minutes. Adding all the potato wedges at once will lower the temperature of the oil, making the potatoes oily.

Remove the potato wedges to a plate covered with kitchen paper, set aside and keep warm. Season to taste.

Pommes Purée

An upmarket potato mash that will complement any meat or fish dish. Serve wherever you would use old-fashioned mashed potato.

1 kg desiree potatoes, washed, skin left on

200 ml milk

250 g unsalted butter

Sea salt and white pepper, to season

To prepare the pommes purée, place the potatoes on a large baking tray and roast until soft. This will take about 1 ½ to 2 hours. Remove and cool slightly. When the potatoes are cool enough to handle, cut in half and scoop out the flesh into a large saucepan.

Place a small saucepan over medium heat, add milk and butter. Slowly bring to the boil. Slowly add the butter and milk mixture to the potato flesh. Mash until smooth and creamy. Season to taste.

Pommes Salardaise

Don't be afraid of using duck fat — it actually has less cholesterol than butter and gives these potatoes a golden, crispy coating. Serve these potatoes with rich dishes such as duck confit, roast chicken or turkey, even omelettes for a fresh take on 'egg and chips'.

250 g pink-eye potatoes
50 g duck fat
100 g button mushroom, finely sliced
1 teaspoon fresh garlic puree
1 teaspoon finely chopped rosemary leaves
Small bunch flat leaf parsley, finely chopped
Sea salt and white pepper, to season

Preheat the oven to 220° C.

Place a large double-boiler saucepan over high heat. Add the potatoes and steam for 20 minutes. Remove and when cool enough to handle, peel and cut the potatoes into large dice.

Place a large heavy-based frying pan over high heat and melt the duck fat. Add the diced potatoes and toss through the fat until golden. Remove and place on a baking tray. Add the mushrooms to the pan and cook until golden. Then add the garlic and herbs, cooking for a further 1 to 2 minutes. Remove the mushroom mixture from the pan and sprinkle over the potatoes. Place the baking tray into and cook for about 20 minutes or until crispy. Remove from oven, season and serve.

Rice Pilaf

This is a versatile rice dish that you can use in place of steamed rice.

2 tablespoons olive oil

200 g butter, cut into cubes

$^1/_2$ cup white wine

500 g jasmine rice

1 litre chicken or veal stock, boiling

$^1/_2$ white onion, finely diced

$^1/_2$ tablespoon minced garlic

Preheat oven to 180°C (350°F).

To prepare the rice, place an ovenproof baking dish over medium heat. Add the oil and half the butter. Add the onion and the garlic and cook for 1 minute, add the wine and reduce by half. Add the rice and stir well to coat all the grains of rice with oil. Pour in the hot stock, stir and cover with foil. Place in oven and bake for 18 minutes.

Remove from the oven, fluff up with a fork and stir through the rest of the butter. Keep warm until ready to serve.

Bitton – striving for success

Bitton, the business, started as a small dream and it has become something much bigger than Sohani and myself ever imagined. From the humble beginnings of a little coffee shop to looking at where Bitton is today makes me realise how far we have come. There are now 12 products stocked in over 450 stores all over Australia and internationally. We have made a name for ourselves, creating a beautiful café and grocer for customers to come and enjoy.

Not only has the business been running for 10 years (and hopefully many more), we have been richly rewarded with the wonderful relationships we have made and maintained. Community and people contribute greatly to our success. Bitton is more than a café. It is a place where the locals have embraced our business — our customers are the heart and foundation of the warm, friendly environment that Bitton Café and Grocer represents.

This connection to community and to the customers is a reflection of my personal ideals. From very early on in my career as a chef I loved meeting people. Talking and learning from others is what gets me excited, dealing with people daily at the café is the thing that makes me greet each day with eagerness and excitement. No day is ever the same. Coming out of my love of dealing with people comes the desire to give back to a community that has supported my family and me for so many years. Working at Bitton feels like a second home — both the staff and the customers — give me perspective on what is happening in the world outside my own. When Bitton first opened I promised myself I would always give back to the people who have supported me from the beginning. I strive to find ways to give back, or at least, to balance my karma.

Running a business is demanding, and in the early days we faced the difficulties of finding loyal staff, competing for business with established cafes and financial hardship. What kept us to the path was the determination to never give up and to keep strongly focused on the type of business we wanted to create. We made all the mistakes imaginable when Bitton Café started up but if you don't make mistakes you will never learn from them. Whenever you start up a new venture it seems that people fail to plan, not plan to fail. Another insight was recognising the resources available and the skills of the people around you, honing your attention on your customers, maintaining the passion for what you do and the sky is the limit. You can reach for whatever you dream of.

David Bitton

In business and in life, it is important to have mentors and I have been fortunate enough to be guided and supported by a number of special people who have generously given their time and invaluable business knowledge. I am also a member of The Entrepreneurs Organization (EO) a dynamic global network that enables young entrepreneurs to learn and grow from each other, encouraging greater business success and an enriched personal life. My customers have also taught me a thing or two! Key to being a success in anything you do is sharing experiences with others — you never know when you will come across some nugget of information that seems to appear just when you need it. I always aim to be open to the ideas and advice of others — another key factor in Bitton's success.

Being responsible for your own business can be overwhelming and, at times, threatens to overtake your personal life. In a lifetime averaging 75 years there are 650,000 hours available to us all, keeping that in mind, time is ticking and every minute needs to be lived in the present moment. A balance of work and life is vital. I am fortunate that my business allows me to combine both my working life and my social life. The café has become a meeting place where I have developed a connection with my customers, who have also become my friends. I strongly feel that life is enriched by the memories of time spent with family and friends.

Bitton

Testimonials

'Moroccan paste ... mmmmm ... black olive tapenade ... mmmm ... Thanks for coming to Australia, David.'

John Newton, Food journalist

'Grinders Coffee has developed a warm and enduring relationship with David Bitton over the last 10 years. David is highly regarded as a professional and an innovative leader of Sydney's burgeoning café scene. We congratulate him on his first cookbook.'

Andrew Cannone, NSW State Manager, Grinders Coffee

'I first met David when I arrived as General Manager of Sheraton on the Park in Sydney in 1994. I noticed immediately that he was always full of ideas and enthusiasm in his position as Head Chef of the Gekko Restaurant. He would appear at my office unannounced full of creative energy. One day, he said he had an idea to publish a book. Regretfully, it has taken ten years for his dream to be realised but believe me, as you enjoy this French-inspired café cookbook, it will have been well worth the wait.'

Peter Thompson, General Manager, Four Points Hotels

'I began my food experience with Bitton when I needed some cooking lessons before appearing on *Masterchef*. I believe the Bitton brand is a credit to the food industry and the best part about my experience was undoubtedly the generous, fun and professional team I was lucky enough to work beside. Brekky on Sunday at Bitton? Yes please!'

Rachel Finch, Miss Universe contestant, model, TV presenter

'The delight of the shared experience of creating and enjoying food is fundamental to our wellbeing. Food is to be shared ... the experience of creation is to be shared ... what a wonderful thing that David brings for us all to share — the traditions of his family ... thank you.'

Naomi Simson, Founder and CEO, RedBalloon.com.au

'The best tapenade ... outside the south of France.'

Helen Greenwood, *Good Living, SMH*

'It was 15 years ago that I had the pleasure of meeting this very ambitious, motivated young French chef. After my first introduction, I knew Australia had just received a great culinary asset to its shores. David's enthusiasm, passion for food and entrepreneurial skills have enabled him to be in the position that he is in today and guarantee his success for the future. Thank you David for your contribution and dedication to the hospitality industry.'

George P. Manettas, Director, Goodbran

'David is a true inspiration to any businessman; not only is he switched on, he is always willing to help and guide others — something that he is as passionate about as his food. His enthusiasm to succeed and do the best in all aspects of his life, is a true credit to him and it certainly explains why his is the best strawberry & vanilla jam in the world!'

James Stevens, CEO, Roses Only

'What do you get when you infuse a 5-star restaurant with a local community café? Voila Bittons! Merci Beaucoup David.'

Peter Mansour, CEO, Mansours

'Nothing beats coming home from a long tour and enjoying a meal at my favourite café. A friendly welcome, warm ambience, great coffee and my favourite tomato and goat's cheese on wood-fired toast ... it doesn't get better than that.'

Benn Robinson, Wallabies player

'I have seen David's hard work and dedication turn a small local café, that I happened to stop and have breakfast in one day, into a well respected and rapidly growing business. It has been a pleasure, as a friend and a mentor, to watch his business go from strength to strength. I wish him all the very best for the future.'

John McGrath, CEO, McGrath

Testimonials

Menu Ideas

Celebration Breakfast

Poached Eggs with Tasmanian Smoked Salmon, Baby Spinach
on Roesti Potato with Hollandaise Sauce (page 30)
French Toast à la Bitton with Fresh Strawberries and Orange Jelly (page 36)

Stay in Bed Breakfast

Banana Muffins with French Butter and Strawberry and Vanilla Jam (page 18)
Three Cheese Omelette with Organic Ham (page 28)
Sautéed Forest Mushrooms on Toasted Brioche Gratinated with Gruyére Cheese (page 24)

Light and Healthy Breakfast

Chilli Scrambled Eggs with Wood-fired Bread (page 20)
Home-made Granola with European-style Yoghurt,
Fresh Berries and Orange Jelly (page 22)

Bitton

Taste of Summer Lunch

Grilled Scallops with Balsamic Vinegar, Parmesan and Asparagus (page 52)

Glazed Quail with Spiced Apple Stir-fry (page 68)

Exotic Fruit Salad with Lemongrass Broth and Ginger Ice Cream (page 162)

Quick and Impressive Lunch for the Girls

Prawn Cocktail (page 42)

Orriechetta with Lemon Zest, Basil and Chilli Garlic Masala (page 112)

Strawberry, Lime and Basil Mousse (page 136)

Relaxed Café Lunch at Home

Salad of Chevre, Beetroot, Green Beans and Baby Rocket with Lemon Dressing (page 74)

Wagyu Beef Burger with Pickled Vegetables (page 94)

Pommes Frites (page 200)

Bitton's Tiramisu (page 158)

Menu Ideas

Spicy Sunday Roast

Chilli and Garlic Roasted Chicken with Caramelised Vegetables (page 126)

Bread and Butter Pudding with Crème Anglaise (page 146)

Casual Dinner Party with Friends

Salmon Braised in Spicy Tomato Sauce (page 124)

Rice Pilaf (page 206)

Green Salad with French Vinaigrette (page 174)

Baked Mango and Ginger Cheesecake (page 160)

Elegant Dinner Party

Smoked Salmon with Crab and Celeriac Rémoulade and Green Shallot Dressing (page 72)

Spiced Milk-fed Veal with Kumara Tart, Golden Shallots and Fresh Pea Sauce (page 100)

Apple Tart (page 152)

Warming Winter Dinner

Soupe a L'oignon (page 54)

Peppered Beef Eye Fillet with Pommes Frites and Red Wine Sauce (page 84)

Poached Pear with Gratinated Blue Cheese and Cayenne Pepper (page 164)

Classic French

Duck Salad with Witlof, Endive and Walnuts (page 44)

Crispy Skin Barramundi with Celeriac Purée and Onion Salsa (page 96)

French Crepes with Vanilla Bean Ice Cream and Orange Jelly (page 142)

Weekday Dinner

Mushroom and vanilla cappuccino soup (page 62)

Moroccan-spiced Lamb with Preserved Lemon Risotto (page 104)

French Crepes with Vanilla Bean Ice Cream and Orange Jelly (page 142)

Menu Ideas

Index

Index

Acknowledgements

Bitton is a collaboration of many great minds bringing ideas and fresh approaches to the business. Over the years, many people have contributed to the 'flavour' of Bitton, making it what it is today, driving it towards an exciting and dynamic future.

Thanks go to my family — Mum, Dad and my brothers Michel and Franck. Your love and encouragement, not to mention my food memories, have intrinsically shaped my food philosphy.

My in-laws — Mr and Mrs Singh and Avanti have welcomed me into their family. Thank you for your ongoing support and guidance, and for your love, generosity and kindness.

To Brad Hamilton, Laurent Curvat, Herve Busson, Olivier Foussat, David Bramley, Ashley Singh-Browne, Matthew Hutchings and George Manettas — thank you for being by my side all this time. Your support and friendship has been an inspiration.

In November 2000 when the Bitton products were first started, Five chefs worked around the clock helping me. My thanks go to Kathleen Higgins, David Constantine, Elias Mata, Johnatan Capitaine and Antoine Moscovitz. They would start at midnight, finishing at 5 or 6 in the morning, then go off to their full-time work. I can't thank you all enough — you made the dream a reality.

Gaby Daoud, from day one you have been an unbelievable business partner. Your dedication and commitment are a great support and your feedback, as ever, invaluable.

Camilla Gill, without you this book would never have seen the light of day. Never have I met someone with so much patience and understanding, not to mention our friendship. It would take a page to list all the things you have contributed to develop Bitton over the past six and a half years. You are a rockstar!

And the team — Andy Tran, you give Bitton the buzz, something that would never have happened without your loyal service. Chris Aguasa, thank you for punching above your weight during the days of the

Bitton

book's photoshoot. A big, big thank you to the entire Bitton team who welcome people back with great service and delicious food — every single day.

A special and heartfelt thanks to three very good friends who have all given generously of their time and their wisdom — Paul Cheika for creating the financial foundation for Bitton; Peter Mansour for introducing me to the Entrepreneurs Organization; John McGrath for guiding me every step of the way and helping me to take my business to a completely new level.

My forum group from Entrepreneurs Organization have been an amazing group of entrepreneurs and friends, providing feedback, advice and camaraderie — thank you, guys.

I was fortunate enough to meet Lisa Messenger at a time when the book needed direction and focus. Without her passion and inspired expertise, this book would still be an idea waiting to happen. Thanks to Lisa and her team — Erin Kelly, Claire Livingston and Jennifer Ross.

Thanks to those who helped put this book together — Johan Palsson for his photography, Carolyn Fienberg for her styling for the photoshoot, Anna Beaumont for testing all the recipes, Ellie Exarchos for her design and Jody Lee for editing.

My suppliers — Grinders Coffee, Top Cut Meats, Ramasa Fine Food, Brasserie Bread, Quality Continental Breads, Australia on the plate, Choco Cannelle, Tidine Pty Ltd, Game Farm, Sublime Gelato — have played their part in the building and growing of Bitton. It is a pleasure doing business with you all — here's to many more years.

To my customers who greet me at breakfast, lunch and dinner. Your support is invaluable — you are all part of the Bitton family.

Big kisses also to my children — Monet Maya and Mayen Matisse Bitton — you keep life in perspective.

Last but not least. To the woman who has been by my side for 20 years — without your calm, your patience, your motivation and your love, the road to success would have been a rocky and winding one. You are everything to me.

Acknowledgements

First edition copyright © David Bitton, 2010

www.bittongourmet.com.au

All rights reserved. No part of this book may be reproduced or transmitted in any form by any means, electronic or mechanical, including photocopying, recording or by any information storage or retrieval system, without prior permission in writing from the publisher. The Australian Copyright Act 1968 (the Act) allows a maximum of one chapter or 10 per cent of the book, whichever is the greater, to be photocopied by any educational institution for its educational purposes provided that the educational institution (or body that administers it) has given a remuneration notice to Copyright Agency Limited (CAL) under the Act.

A CIP catalogue of this book is available from the National Library of Australia.

ISBN: 978-0-9808097-0-1

Edited by Jody Lee
Photography by Johan Palsson
Styling by Carolyn Fienberg
Design by Ellie Exarchos
Project management, marketing and print
 management by The Messenger Group

Conversions: All measurements are metric
1 teaspoon = 5 ml
1 tablespoon = 20 ml

www.themessengergroup.com.au

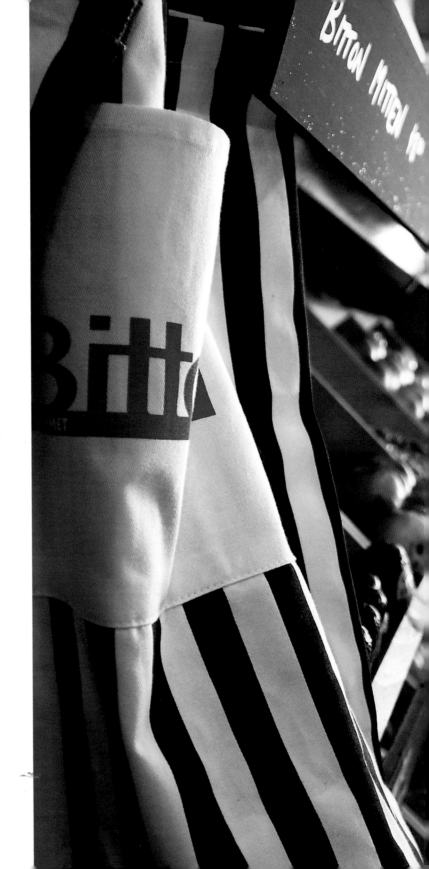